LEADING MEDICAID MANAGED CARE PLANS

A State Relationship Perspective

LEADING MEDICAID MANAGED CARE PLANS

A State Relationship Perspective

Arlene Davidson

CRC Press
Taylor & Francis Group

CRC Press is an imprint of the
Taylor & Francis Group, an **informa** business

A PRODUCTIVITY PRESS BOOK

CRC Press
Taylor & Francis Group
6000 Broken Sound Parkway NW, Suite 300
Boca Raton, FL 33487-2742

© 2018 by Taylor & Francis Group, LLC

CRC Press is an imprint of Taylor & Francis Group, an Informa business

No claim to original U.S. Government works

Printed on acid-free paper

International Standard Book Number-13: 978-1-138-30375-1 (Hardback)
International Standard Book Number-13: 978-1-138-30373-7 (Paperback)
International Standard Book Number-13: 978-0-203-73076-8 (eBook)

Library of Congress Cataloging-in-Publication Data

Names: Davidson, Arlene, 1956- author.
Title: Leading Medicaid managed care plans : a state relationship perspective / Arlene Davidson.
Description: Boca Raton : Taylor & Francis, [2018] | Includes bibliographical references and index.
Identifiers: LCCN 2017023916| ISBN 9781138303737 (pbk. : alk. paper) | ISBN 9781138303751 (hardback : alk. paper) | ISBN 9780203730768 (ebook)
Subjects: | MESH: Medicaid | Managed Care Programs | State Government | United States
Classification: LCC RA412.4 | NLM W 250 AA1 | DDC 368.4/200973--dc23
LC record available at https://lccn.loc.gov/2017023916.

Visit the Taylor & Francis Web site at
http://www.taylorandfrancis.com

and the CRC Press Web site at
http://www.crcpress.com

To Rick M. Jelinek and Phyllis Biedess,
mentors who taught me all I know and had faith in my abilities.

To Joette Bober, who taught me what I didn't know
and whose faith in me is unwavering.

Contents

Acknowledgments

My career succeeded through the help of others and writing this book was a similar experience. I could not have done it without the review and suggestions of the following learned individuals: Christy Harris Lemak, PhD, FACHE, professor and chair, Health Service administration, School of Health Professions, University of Alabama at Birmingham, who pointed me in the right directions; the expert critique of John R. Griffith, professor emeritus, Department of Health Management and Policy, University of Michigan School of Public Health, who challenged me on several occasions and in several ways which all led to vast improvements in the final product; and the support and recommendations of Phyllis Biedess, former director of the Arizona Health Care Cost Containment System (AHCCCS, the state's Medicaid program). Also to Rick Jelinek and Elizabeth Cabot Nash, who provided critical information and ideas. To the following people who additionally contributed to getting this book published: Marilyn Greco, Rick Hamilton, Maria C. Speth, Bill Anger, Bob Crawford, my editorial assistant Alexandria Gryder, senior editor, Kristine Mednansky, and of course, Joette. And finally to Arlene Elliott, MHSA, who read the earliest version and provided me much needed support and confidence to move forward. To all I owe a great debt of gratitude.

Author

 **Arlene Davidson**, MHSA, is a health care consultant, author and lecturer with over 37 years of experience in Medicaid and acute managed care health plans, health insurance organizations and hospitals. She specializes in working with CEOs and other leaders in turning around struggling companies and in securing multi-billion dollar contracts. She works with organizations in mission and vision development, strategic planning, customer relationships, business development and communication strategies. Her career has included executive positions with large multi-national health care companies as well as consulting firms, regional managed care plans and hospitals. Ms. Davidson holds a master of health services administration from the University of Michigan and a bachelor of science in business from Arizona State University.

Introduction

Leading a Medicaid health plan can be a rewarding challenge. Done well, it is a unique opportunity to positively influence the health of our society's most vulnerable citizens—the poor, disabled, acute and chronically ill individuals of all ages enrolled in Medicaid and living in all areas of the United States. It is an opportunity to excel, via state contractual relationships, in which private–public collaboration benefits the common good and advances the health of those people entrusted to you as leaders of Medicaid health plans. Done poorly, it can be a nightmare that no health plan executive or state Medicaid director wants to experience.

This book is written from the perspective of both extremes—I have witnessed health plan management done well and worked tirelessly to save those who were managed poorly. This is for executives and managers of Medicaid managed care health plans (the specific population or model does not matter; whether acute care, long-term care, Children's Health Insurance Plans or Primary Care Case Management, etc.) who wish to do it well or even better than well. Being successful at Medicaid managed care is not simply satisfying the members of your health plan, although that is an important goal. And it is not simply pleasing whoever is director of your state's Medicaid department, although that also is an important goal. It takes relentless focus on your "main customer," and first understanding who that is. Your "main customer" is the state Medicaid or health care agency and the executives and administrators responsible for its successful operation. They desire quality health care for their state's most vulnerable population and they want it at minimum cost. This main customer concept extends to your state's governor, legislative health care committees and commissions, health policy advocacy groups, and health care lobbyists. It requires your dedication to a fiduciary responsibility to the state along with a core value of stewardship and accountability in executing your Medicaid contract successfully. It is establishing a culture that values meaningful relationships with your state, members, providers and employees and applying that to the daily discipline of managing the business. It can be exhilarating work, but make no mistake, it is *hard* work.

During my 37 years in health care, I've spent over 24 years in the managed care industry and most of those in the Medicaid arena. I've worked with various chief executive officers and their staff in health plans locally owned or part of mid-to-large national companies, with memberships ranging from 50,000 to over 400,000, and annual revenues in the millions to billions. The successful ones all shared similar attributes:

- Close state relationships that were described (by the state) as collaborative, trustworthy and respectful
- Consistency, overtime, in meeting or exceeding state contractual requirements
- Few state imposed sanctions or penalties
- Health plan leadership described as humble, honest, transparent and focused
- Health plan has high employee satisfaction survey scores and low staff turnover
- High member satisfaction survey scores
- Solid and supportive community relationships
- Financially stable (i.e., meeting internal budget requirements as well as state financial requirements)

Not surprisingly, those health plans in trouble also shared similar attributes with each other:

- Broken, or in some cases, non-existent state relationships that were described (by both the state and health plan leaders) as adversarial, confrontational, "us against them" and health plan leadership seen as arrogant, rigid or clueless
- Health plan's continuous failure to meet key contractual requirements, which resulted in frequent issuance of state sanctions and penalties
- High number of provider and/or member complaints
- Low health plan employee satisfaction survey scores and high staff turnover
- Financially unstable (e.g., not meeting internal budget requirements)

Individually, these were organizations in severe trouble with their respective states; under threat of enrollment sanctions to out-right contractual cancellation. Rescuing these organizations took enormous effort by many people and this book provides examples of successful turnarounds. It wasn't simply replacing a few top leaders. It was rebuilding the organization, emphasizing realistic improvements in every aspect of operations, but particularly key state Medicaid contractual requirements such as claims payments, turnaround times on appeals, report submissions, and more. In some cases the top leader was excellent but the health plan was still failing—a signal that the CEO had probably inherited an unskilled management team. The first time I experienced this, I was ready to toss the CEO; it was a lesson that even the most gifted CEO still needs good, capable people around them.

I often wondered, how did things get so bad? Why did the same issues linger, sometimes for years? The far majority of issues uncovered, and subsequently fixed, struck me as "Basic Management 101." Few people knew the contractual requirements from the state, so reports were incomplete and deadlines were frequently missed. There were few if any operational meetings in which health plan executives and managers reviewed reports on—what seemed to me as everyday routine activities—like reviewing hospital census, claims reports, compliance reports or finances. The reports themselves were rarely reviewed by anyone, so operational issues were not identified or rectified. There were no cross-departmental meetings so, for example, provider services never heard about the complaints received by member services regarding certain providers, or that clinical management was struggling with providers who had just inked generous contracts with the health plan. Meetings with the state were contentious but also informative—if the health plan staff attending had been listening. The state Medicaid staff were quite clear what the health plan needed to do, it's just that no one did it, increasing the state's level of frustration and the decibel level of their voices of discontent.

And yet, for every health plan reversed from poor-performing to excelling, my colleagues and I involved in the turnaround emerged each time better prepared, better positioned and having learned valuable lessons. Some of these lessons are: it is a lot easier to maintain and sustain good leadership and management practices rather than continuously parachute in to failing health plans and performing emergency rescue missions—they are stressful, soul-draining and financially expensive. And risky.

The commonalities between the health plans doing well (or not doing well) had a lot to do with their cultures. The successful health plans had trustful relationships with the state, and recognized and treated them as their main customer as well as healthy relationships with providers, members, employees and the community. They had a relentless focus on delivering excellence throughout the organization; were humble enough to ask the state for help when needed (most states are remarkably open and responsive to helping their contracted health plans be successful); demonstrated integrity in their business interactions with the state, providers and other stakeholders. They had cultures of discipline but also knew how to have fun and to celebrate achievements, no matter how small.

A notion I introduce in this book is the aspiration of delighting your state Medicaid agency. Rather than adversaries, it is possible to be collaborators in the pursuit of a common mission, as explored in Chapter 1. There are four ideals of Medicaid managed care:

1. States who wish to fulfill their mission and public mandates with reasonable budgets
2. Health plans who wish to pursue their missions and meet operational and financial targets
3. Providers who wish to attain professional aspirations with reasonable reimbursements
4. Members who desire access to needed health care services to improve well-being and to be treated with dignity and respect

These ideals or concepts are held together by contracts and meeting those contractual requirements is a major theme of this book, especially the contract you hold with your state Medicaid agency.

Some of the examples used in this book are the result of a composite health plan. I've combined some of the health plans into one, for the sake of protecting the identities of states and/or the leaders of health plans, some of whom are still active in their careers. The purpose of this book is to educate and inspire, not to embarrass those who fell short of the mark nor to create celebrities of those who excelled, but to propel each of us to do better and to advance the value of sustainable state agency relationships.

My mission is to help you understand what elements are needed for a successful Medicaid health plan and a sustainable relationship with the people in your state Medicaid agency. Any misrepresentations in this book are my own. And in some cases the scope of this book cannot address details around creating mission, vision, values or developing winning cultures, or developing stellar member outreach programs—there are plenty of companies and consultants and books to assist you and in many cases I have listed resources at the end of the book.

The book is divided into two parts. Part I deals with the infrastructure and foundation I believe is necessary to deliver superior services to your customers (i.e., the state, health plan members, etc.) and meet—even exceed—contractual requirements and expectations. Part II delves into more of the details of developing and sustaining relationships with your state Medicaid agency with a long-term, mutually beneficial partnership as the goal.

BUILDING A STRONG FOUNDATION

Chapter 1

Mission, Vision and Values

Whole books and college courses are dedicated to creating and sustaining viable mission, vision and values statements. My objective here is not to repeat what many expert authors have already covered but to underscore the importance of having meaningful mission, vision and values statements and why these are necessary in today's Medicaid and business environment. When I have examined organizations that stumbled and failed, whether non-profit or for-profit, it is often due to a failure to adhere to their founding principles, albeit in addition to subjects covered in the following chapters. The point is, long-lasting success has a better chance of occurring if you start with a strong foundation upon which to build. Like most steps in the creative process, it starts with a main question.

Why Medicaid?

What drives a company to be in the Medicaid managed care business? Why are you involved in Medicaid managed care?

For many companies and individuals, whether non-profit or for-profit, it is to fulfill a desire to help those in need, to assist the less fortunate and to create healthier lives for them or to improve their well-being. Quite often there are strong altruistic elements in these desires, without concern for financial profit or organizational growth. For other institutions, they are focused more on providing value to a variety of stakeholders, including investors for large for-profits, as well as to their employees and contracted providers.

Whatever their motivations, it seems being involved in the Medicaid business lends itself to determining some type of purpose or mission, some over-arching credo that helps explain why people devote themselves to this line of work, aside from collecting a paycheck. I am initially addressing the purpose of Medicaid and the reasons companies (and states) invest so much of themselves in it.

Why the Medicaid program exists in the first place may be a good place to start. Medicaid was signed into law in 1965 and was originally designed to help with the medical expenses of parents and dependent children receiving public assistance and also for aged, blind and disabled individuals. It has expanded in the last 50 years to occupy a major place in America's health care system, to cover more uninsured and underinsured, and the long-term care needs of disabled and/or elderly persons (Paradise *et al.* 2015).

What initially started as a way for our country to address the health care needs of impoverished individuals, has grown into a robust safety-net program with great sources of innovation and health care financing (Paradise *et al.* 2015). Medicaid has also evolved in its *raison d'être*, a sort of "mission creep." Beyond just providing health care services to vulnerable populations, states with Medicaid managed care programs have matured and expanded their missions to encompass a broader spectrum of purpose and many Medicaid health plans need to expand their own missions to address this widening need. Some of Medicaid program expansion was necessary during the years of the Great Recession; other growth was spurred on by the passage of the Affordable Care Act in 2010.

The Medicaid program itself exists as a safety net for our country's most vulnerable and disenfranchised people. The program provides health and long-term care coverage to almost 76 million Americans who are impoverished, in poor mental and or physical health, disabled, lacking social supports and the most unfortunate suffer all of these attributes. Over half of these beneficiaries are enrolled in managed care Medicaid health plans, a program strategy employed by 39 states and the District of Columbia (Medicaid Health Plans of America 2016). The remaining states use non-managed care strategies, or a hybrid, to coordinate health care services for their constituents. The focus of this book is on the states with managed care systems and programs.

Providing health and long-term care coverage to these individuals is complex and expensive. Over $430 billion of combined federal and state Medicaid funding was spent in 2013, with Medicaid typically ranking second in state budgets (Paradise *et al.* 2015). States, who report certain detailed information, paid over $123 billion to managed care organizations in 2013 (The Henry J. Kaiser Family Foundation 2015). For managed care organizations, Medicaid has long been known to have thinner profit margins than other lines of business. Some Medicaid managed care plans are functioning with an average of 0.0% to 1.0% operating profit ratio; some even less (Centers for Medicare and Medicaid Services 2012).

With complex, costly care and narrow profit margins, it is a wonder that people continue to devote themselves to this line of work. This brings us back to my earlier comment about a sense of purpose that drives individuals, and the companies they work for, to pursue or to remain in the Medicaid managed care profession.

Mission, Vision and Values: A State Perspective

Over the years, as Medicaid managed care grew and matured throughout the country, state departments that ran these programs began to mirror other industry organizational trends in developing mission, vision and values statements. Some states created Medicaid dedicated mission statements of what they wished to accomplish; other states added vision statements to further outline to their constituents what they strive to be or what they wish to pursue. Still others have incorporated values statements or principles and ideals, which guide peoples' actions and behaviors (Abrahams 1999). Still other states have separate mission, vision and values statements; and some combine them into one powerful declaration of purpose. The oft repeated dictum of "if you've seen one Medicaid program, you've seen one Medicaid program" applies equally to their operational design as to their creation of mission statements.

Here are some examples, easily available on each state's publicly accessible websites:

CALIFORNIA MEDI-CAL MANAGED CARE DIVISION

Mission: The mission of the California Department of Health Services is to protect and improve the health of all Californians.

Vision: All Medi-Cal managed care enrollees will have access to health care which is safe, effective, patient-centered, timely, efficient and equitable, and which serves to reduce the burden of illness and improve the health and functioning of the enrolled individuals and population.

(From public domain at www.dhcs.ca.gov/Medi-cal)

NEW JERSEY DEPARTMENT OF HUMAN SERVICES

Mission: The Department of Human Services is dedicated to providing quality services that consistently meet expectations with the goal to protect, assist and empower economically disadvantaged individuals and families, and people with disabilities to achieve their maximum potential. We strive to ensure a seamless array of services through partnerships and collaborations with communities statewide. We seek to promote accountability, transparency and quality in all that we do.

(From public domain at www.state.nj.us/Medicaid)

PENNSYLVANIA DEPARTMENT OF HUMAN SERVICES

Vision: To see Pennsylvanians living safe, healthy and independent lives.

Mission: To improve the quality of life for Pennsylvania's individuals and families. We promote opportunities for independence through services and supports while demonstrating accountability for taxpayer resources.

Values: Collaboration, communication, accountability, respect and effectiveness.

(From public domain at www.dhs.pa.gov/Medicaid)

The way states display their mission statements is equally varied. Some post them visibly on their websites, as shown above.

Other states incorporate their mission or purpose into annual reports or strategic plans. For example, the State of Tennessee and its Bureau of TennCare, their Medicaid managed care program, combined a mission (what it wants to accomplish) with a vision (what to pursue) in its cover letter of a recent annual report:

> The Bureau of TennCare strives to provide health care to Tennessee's most vulnerable population in a way that meets high quality standards while remaining cost effective in the process. [...] Continuing to create more long-term care options for the state's

elderly and adults with physical disabilities […] our dedicated staff will continue to pursue opportunities to improve administrative operations and quality of care for our members.

Adapted from public domain at www.tn.gov/TennCare

The State of Arizona's Medicaid program—the Arizona Health Care Cost Containment System or AHCCCS—publishes its mission in several places, but most prominently in its 2015 five-year strategic plan.

ARIZONA HEALTH CARE COST CONTAINMENT SYSTEM

Vision: Shaping tomorrow's managed health care […] from today's experience, quality and innovation.

Mission: Reaching across Arizona to provide comprehensive, quality health care for those in need.

(From public domain at www.azahcccs.gov)

Mission, Vision and Values: A Health Plan Perspective

Managed care companies evolved right along with the states in creating mission, vision and value statements as foundations on which to build their futures. Here are some examples from national Medicaid companies which can also be accessed on their corporate websites.

UNITEDHEALTH GROUP

Mission: Our mission is to help people live healthier lives and to help make the health system work better for everyone.

Values: Integrity, compassion, relationships, innovation, performance.

(From 2016 Annual Report at www.unitedhealthgroup.com)

AMERIGROUP

Purpose: Together, we are transforming health care with trusted and caring solutions.

Vision: To be America's valued health partner.

Values: Trustworthy, accountable, innovative, caring, easy to do business with.

(From 2017 www.amerigroup.com/aboutus)

These examples of managed care companies only reflect large, national organizations, but there are numerous regional and local managed care health plans with similar statements of purpose and vision.

Several things are clear in reviewing all of these statements and those of entities not listed here: states with Medicaid managed care programs, and health care companies that contract with them, want to protect or help those less fortunate and to improve or transform their health or the health care system itself. Those that list values commonly cite similar principles: compassion, integrity, accountability and respect. Comparing these statements across states as well as across managed care companies reveals more commonality than differences. We are more in alignment with each other than many other business relationships, and this reveals an opportunity that seems seldom realized.

Aligning State and Health Plan Perspectives

Why aren't managed care companies more attuned to assisting states in realizing their missions and reaching their visions? Would it be so outlandish if a managed care organization actually had that in their own mission statement—to assist states in improving the health of their Medicaid beneficiaries? Why not help states—as our main customer—to achieve their goals?

Perhaps some organizations are not ready to put such language into their own mission statements, but that doesn't mean the conversation can't take place between managed care leadership and state leadership. I have seen the response from state leadership when the leader(s) of contracted health plans begin the conversation of wanting to assist the state in meeting their stated goals and objectives, or the willingness to partner with a state in pursuing mutual missions and visions. The response from states varies; from skepticism (this is new to them, a signal that no one else has offered to think of the state as a priority) to surprised; but most often it is positive and even accompanied by a sense of relief. I say relief because rather than a confrontational, adversarial relationship, a true partnership emerges where both parties stand to gain and most importantly, Medicaid recipients benefit from the mutual alignment of the dual purpose of these private-public partnerships. One caveat to having this kind of discussion with your state is the condition of your working relationship with your Medicaid agency. You have to have some credibility as a well-performing health plan before embarking on this conversation. If you are in trouble with your state due to performance issues, read Chapter 5, Creating Lasting State Relationships, before meeting to discuss mission, vision and values.

Our goal(s) shouldn't just be to hit certain revenue or net income numbers, certain medical management metrics or just increase our market share; those are all fine goals to strive for, but to what end? What ultimate outcome? If we truly believe in our missions, then we equally are interested in having an impact on the health of the communities in which we do business, in the states that we are contracted with. How do we achieve that? By understanding our states' missions, as well as their desires and constraints, and then organizing around what we have in common to working toward those goals. In other words, your managed care company's annual goals include items that your state wants/needs to achieve.

It is possible to create and pursue mission, vision and values and achieve balanced budgets, or as Timothy Egan states in his April 8th, 2017 *New York Times* article "The Soul of a Corporation," "that a higher purpose with a solid bottom line does not have to be an oxymoron." I believe, as Egan does, that corporations can achieve financial success and business objectives without losing their soul or breaching ethical standards. We mostly hear in the press about corporations behaving badly, such as health care companies committing fraud (typically against Medicaid or Medicare) or companies trying to cheat the law (such as Volkswagen with emission testing) or violating acceptable office behavior (such as Fox News and its numerous sexual harassment settlements). There are equally a number of organizations that retain their corporate moral compass, meet their strategic goals and objectives, and provide value to their stakeholders. Egan cites, in his *New York Times* article, companies like REI and Patagonia that are thriving while other retailers are struggling. What sets REI and Patagonia apart is their steadfast adherence to their missions and a set of ethical values. To this I add health care companies like Aetna and UnitedHealth Group, for example, whose corporate missions to serve others is concomitant with business and financial growth and success.

I once served as a board member of an organization that had just gone through a robust 12-month process of creating its five-year strategic plan, within which were the mission, vision and values statements. We had gathered at a board meeting in which the organization's chief executive was to review with us the final draft. This executive, with albeit good intentions, had changed the mission and vision statements without any input from the board. I was quite surprised and shared my concerns that no organization should be changing its mission and vision without board input and certainly not after spending a year developing a five-year strategic plan which utilized the mission as guidance. Everyone agreed to leave the mission and vision statements as previously written, as there was no time to revise those and the strategic plan and have any hope of reaching any of our current year goals and objectives. It all underscored the importance of a board (particularly the chair) working closely with its executive(s) and leaders and having clarity around roles, responsibilities and expectations (more on this later), and a regular review of an organization's mission and vision. No rogue board member or staff member should be re-writing by themselves an organization's main purpose for existing.

Who exactly writes the mission statement? Ideally, this should be a group activity involving the board and senior leaders of the organization, for example, the C-suite (chief executive officer, chief operating officer, chief medical officer, chief financial officer, etc.) with input from employees at all levels of the company. This group's composition can vary and may include a subcommittee of board members with a select group of senior leaders and other staff, who bring to the full board examples of what they created. Senior management is generally responsible for determining that a mission statement needs review, refreshment or updating, based on organizational growth and/or a change in direction, etc. Senior management also sets the process—who is involved, time limits on the process and the roll-out of a new mission statement. Many organizations also take this time to create or re-evaluate vision and values statements. One step I have found to be enormously helpful is looking at other organization's mission statements (which is why I have included some starter examples in this book) and also background articles or books, such as Abrahams' *The Mission Statement Book.*

A Word about Culture

Mission, vision and values shape an organization's identity, provides a compass for all stakeholders to know what direction you are headed and serves to unify employees, members, providers and others. They are also helpful as a touch-stone to return to when your organization ends up in trouble—returning to your reason for being clarifies and simplifies, helps leaders separate the chafe from the wheat and focus on critical goals and strategies. I find it useful to review (this does not necessarily mean revise) an organization's mission, vision and values statements annually, as part of the strategic planning process.

Solid mission, vision and values statements also contribute to your organization's culture. Culture can be described as the "collective habits and behaviors of all the teams and individuals that make up the organization" (Senn and Hart 2010). Winning cultures look and feel the same—you and your employees are accountable, collaborative, creative, positive, hopeful and effective. They apply the "culture of discipline" as described in Jim Collins' book *Good to Great* (Harper Business, 2001). Results-oriented and success-ful organizations are more likely to be associated with higher goals—that is, mission, vision and values statements. One description I have heard (but can-not cite) is "culture is values in action everyday." In the context of this book, this means focusing on achieving results that meet or exceed state contrac-tual requirements; treating state Medicaid leaders and staff with dignity and respect—ideals that are expanded on later in this book.

The point is to start with clear mission, vision and value statements. Review them regularly (at least annually) to anchor and focus your team. Discuss them with your state counterparts to ensure you are in alignment on key elements. Refer to them to guide your strategic planning. When organi-zations start to go off course and experience failure, quite often it is because they lost their true north and deviated from their main purpose.

Summary of Key Points

- Know and understand your state's Medicaid mission, vision and value statements; if not readily available, search directors' statements, annual reports, strategic plans, governors' speeches or simply ask them.
- Create or revise your own mission, vision and values statements with a clear and inclusive process; consider including goals to help your state if practical.

- Develop these in concert with developing a culture of success; author Jim Collins (2001) refers to "greatness is a choice and a discipline."
- Review in meetings with state Medicaid leadership—discover what you have in common, pursue mutual desires to achieve, help your state be successful along with your own health plan and agree with each other on how to measure progress.
- Revisit with your state Medicaid agency regularly (e.g., annually) on agreed-upon time frames.
- Regularly review the above with your employees, so all are involved in developing, revising or reviewing your mission, vision and values statements.

Chapter 2

Governance and Leadership

The Importance of an Effective Board

The best missions and visions will remain unfulfilled without a means to shepherd them and advance them to ensure their realization. The most effective way to achieve your organization's mission is to have a capable leadership team and staff to implement strategic plans that accelerate the mission, and a functional governing board for oversight and support. In this context, governance is achieved by a fully functional and local board of directors who exist as an integral piece of a successful organization, not just as figure-heads or to meet state contractual requirements. Many state Medicaid programs have a vested interest in their managed care contractual health plans' governance and leadership. They want assurances that a body of overseers is monitoring health plan activities and are good stewards of the state's financial payments toward health care services for the members. This notion of governance is also a common question in Request for Proposals (RFP). Most states with competitive RFP processes for Medicaid contract renewal ask questions about who is on the board, how often they meet, what power or authority they have to effectuate change at the health plan, etc. And many states look for community representation on the board and a diversity that reflects the demographics of your health plan's membership, even if not required by state contract.

Many of today's Medicaid health plans are part of larger national or regional corporations, such as Molina, Centene, Anthem, UnitedHealthcare and more. Future mergers of health care companies are to be anticipated and this raises some governance issues between corporate leadership and local boards of that corporation's Medicaid health plans. What state Medicaid agencies are looking for is the ability of the local health plan to have some influence over decisions made at the corporate level that have impact on the local plan's ability to operate effectively. One way of ensuring this is to appoint people from the corporate office to the local board, so they hear first hand what the issues are closer to where they are happening. This has the added benefit of improving communications from the local health plan back to corporate. The common dictum "Medicaid is local" is meant to describe how unique each state is and each Medicaid program. Although state Medicaid programs nationally have more in common than differences, it's knowing and understanding those differences that is key and appropriate governance over those nuances can mean the difference between success and failure.

For local boards, corporate personnel and even corporate board of directors, the lines of communication, reporting structures and decision-making criteria all need to be clear and understood. Do the local boards all report to one corporate executive or to a corporate council? In what ways can local boards escalate urgent issues to corporate? How does a local board make its voice heard and get issues prioritized? I mention these as real-life circumstances that occurred at various health plans I was involved with that dealt with silent corporations. That is, issues were raised by the local unit to corporate leadership, but little to no action was taken and the issue negatively affected operations, which lead to a failure of meeting state Medicaid contractual requirements. A consistent theme in this book is long-term success in this industry is all about meeting contractual requirements.

A critical factor is effective governance and local-to-corporate relationships, and having the structures in place that allow for good communications, escalation of issues and timely action on those issues. For smaller, independent health plans, this may extend to oversight of contractors who manage, for example, claims, call centers or enrollment activities. As part of board governance, make sure health plan personnel execute contracts with these subcontractors that are clear and have measurable expectations and consequences of not meeting those expectations.

A corporate appointee to the local health plan board, and good governance policies, will also help in situations where the large corporation has a subsidiary that ends up doing business with the local health plan's competition. A real-life example: Corporation A is a large multi-faceted health care company with Medicaid health plans in several states, including Health Plan A-1 in state X. Health Plan A-1 is preparing for a Request for Proposal (RFP) to renew its multi-billion-dollar contract with state X. Health Plan B is also in the state of X and is a competitor of Health Plan A-1 and is also preparing for the RFP. A subsidiary of corporation A contracts with Health Plan B to help with financial activities related to B's RFP response. This short-term contract is worth less than $250,000. Health Plan A-1 knows nothing of this and in fact senior executives at corporation A know nothing of this. It is discovered at a state X meeting, necessitating Health Plan A-1 to reveal the conflict of interest, which came across to the state as a lack of appropriate oversight and corporate governance. It nearly jeopardized corporation A's multi-billion-dollar business in state X for the sake of a smaller book of business. So, in addition to good communication and strong relationships between local and corporate offices, good governance also means good communication and relationships across corporate entities. The business development departments in subsidiaries of large corporations need to have some way of communicating across corporate chambers what their potential targets are in the states. Even better is a coordinated approach with customers who overlap. The only way to ensure these activities occur is to have executive leadership support and guidance and effective oversight.

Here's what I mean about these last two comments. In the first, communicating across corporate chambers, this helps avoid the conflict of interest situation mentioned above when one corporate subsidiary's billion dollar book of business was threatened by another subsidiary's $250,000 contract with a competitor during an open procurement process. If the different corporate subsidiaries met regularly and shared business prospects and talked openly about risks and opportunities (and these opportunities include expanding influential relationships), this situation could have been avoided or handled in a way that did not embarrass the entity seeking contract renewal. Second, coordinated approaches by subsidiaries can have a positive additive effect. For example, some national health care companies contract with states for Medicaid as well as commercial insurance for the state's employees. Coordinating the company's approach and meetings with State leaders can be more powerful than creating an atmosphere of corporate business developers peppering state leaders with meeting after meeting. state leaders (e.g., the governor, the governor's health policy advisor, legislators heading health care related committees, etc.) complain about the rotation of the same corporations' executives coming to meet on commercial insurance then another set of executives from the same corporation enter to talk about Medicaid. One state legislator referred to it as a revolving door of "corporate suits"; it was with a tone of annoyance. Why not coordinate these meetings and provide a comprehensive message and approach? This can be accomplished by creating and delivering talking points that portray the all-inclusive capabilities of your corporation while demonstrating awareness and respect for state officials' time constraints. For larger multi-product corporations, this means presenting a cohesive plan of how your company can improve the health of various individuals the state has a vested interest in—its employees and its Medicaid beneficiaries, which comprise the majority of most states' budgets. Again, this is an approach that requires top-down support and oversight. It takes time and effort to coordinate these kind of meetings, and it's easier to default to old ways of doing business. Creating a story of how your corporation can improve the health of its constituents and save the state money can deliver a powerful punch. This also comes with a caveat—if the subsidiary that manages the state's employees' health benefits (typically through a commercial insurance division) and they perform that job poorly, it can have a spill-over effect and negatively impact your Medicaid business in that state; the state's officials do not necessarily look at you separately, but most often consider sister companies from the same corporation as one entity. This "one bad apple spoils the barrel" may not seem fair or even accurate, but it underscores the necessity of effective corporate governance of local business(es) and excellent communications across corporate entities.

Most non-profit or for-profit organizations involved in Medicaid managed care contracts generally have a board of directors who provide strategic direction and guidance to the health plan's CEO. Board members quite often are viewed as "trusted advisors," "nose in, hands off" of day-to-day operations of the business (Larson 2015). An effective board blends fiduciary and legal responsibilities with strategic vision, business skills and expertise, prudent skepticism, judgment and *influence*—not only internally with their working relationship with the CEO but also externally as it relates to stakeholder relationships (especially with the state).

Why is it important to have an effective board? It isn't just for state contractual requirements, as mentioned above, but because you want a sustainable organization that meets its mission, vision and is successful in its execution of its managed care contract(s). This requires thoughtful and capable governance, oversight and leadership.

You also want to avoid the news headline "where was the board?" An executive I once worked for frequently peppered her inspiring and invigorating employee or public talks with "news headlines," as a means to show where we were headed—our collective and desired outcome—as in "General Health Plan ranked number one in the state."

You want to prevent any situation that would embarrass the state and place them in the headlines as a result of your action (or inaction). This is further examined in the chapter on state relationships. Avoiding these headlines is accomplished by effectively executing the duties and key responsibilities of a board as discussed below. This embraces the notion of governance as more than just showing up for a meeting or simply observing while the CEO manages it all, but is actively engaged and thrives in partnership with the CEO, examining ways to avert repeating missteps and methods to strengthen activities that yield positive results.

Key Governance Responsibilities

A proficient board of directors, and effective governance, entails the following (led by the board chair and the organization's chief executive):

- Build a competent board of passionate, committed individuals.
- Establish committee structure, rules of order and procedures.
- Create, evaluate and promote the organization's mission and vision.
- Select, counsel and support the chief executive (and oversight of other key executive positions such as medical officer, finance officer, operating officer, etc.).
- Cultivate a culture of trust and transparency with all stakeholders, including leaders of your state Medicaid managed care program and your health plan employees.
- Approve and ensure effective strategic planning and set direction and policy.
- Employ use of board self-evaluation, performance measurements and benchmarking; apply a balanced scorecard approach.
- Oversee organizational goal setting, benchmarking, assessment and evaluation.
- Listen to interests and form relationships with current and potential stakeholders, including the state, and seek their feedback (in collaboration with the CEO).
- Listen to the interests, form relationships and be involved in the community and bring the community and other stakeholders feedback to attention of full board and staff, and thereby enhance understanding of community needs and promote your public standing and reputation (in collaboration with the CEO).

- Approve major financial decisions, review financial and operational reports.
- Monitor performance as it relates to your state contract and ensure compliance.
- Monitor and strengthen programs and services that enhance the state contract.
- Apply fiduciary judgment and inquiry; ask good questions.
- Ensure resources for all the above.

There are many resources available that expand the detail and provide specifics of additional board roles and responsibilities (a selection of resources is listed at the end of this book). The board of directors is predominately involved in governance policy decisions. These generally are in concert with the chief executive and in case of a national (or regional) company, with corporate executives for guidance and compliance. Most boards spend the majority of their time on strategic thinking—for example, reviewing strategies that create value for the organization and/or the state; engaging in strategies that enhance revenues; growing community collaborations and state relationship(s); answering what changes are needed as the organization grows and expands staff, etc. Boards spend time on mission alignment and advancement, seeking and evaluating new programs that can enhance mission achievement, ensuring compliance with state regulations/contract requirements, and addressing crises and working closely with the company's leaders in appropriately mitigating and avoiding repeating crises.

The board and CEO should be regularly reviewing reports prior to delivery to the state. Set a calendar of meetings for regular review of reports that are submitted to your state (this is dependent on the size of your organization and the level of autonomy given to local leadership; if your health plan is in operational trouble with the state, it behooves you to have governance oversight of this process, that is, involve your board in the review process). Ideally, these meetings should align with state reporting requirements as stated in your contract and health plan leadership should review these for any trends, implement interventions for improvement and then share with the board. Be aware and know when your state is doing their budgeting and strategic planning (and legislative actions) for insights into what might happen to your Medicaid program and schedule your health plan meetings on budgeting and strategic planning accordingly. The board chair and health plan CEO should also meet regularly with the state's Medicaid director and strive to have both executives focused on this relationship. The board chair needs to ensure the CEO is reviewing any reports that come from the state (and their own organization) to monitor any gaps in performance. These gaps and ongoing operational missteps lead to state imposed sanctions, penalties, potentially bad press but most importantly, it can negatively affect your overall relationship with the state.

This raises the question of how often the board should meet, which is quite often dependent on circumstances surrounding the operations of the health plan. Many boards, overseeing solid, mature health plans that are functioning well, meet on a quarterly basis, reflecting confidence in the leadership and management of health plan executives and staff. I have worked with organizations in which the board met monthly; due to excessive growth and large strategic opportunities all occurring at once or due to operational failures necessitating more frequent and closer oversight of health plan activities. It is important to understand your state's view on appropriate governance and adjust your board's meeting frequency and agendas accordingly. States that highly value governance and board involvement generally want to see a minimum of quarterly meetings. I'm not suggesting that state Medicaid agencies have the power or authority to dictate how often your board meets, rather, it is understanding the level of governance and oversight they expect and then meeting that expectation. This may be achieved by demonstrating to the state the board's involvement in strategic planning, review of critical business decisions or addressing issues of importance to the state.

Cultivating and nurturing relationships may be a board responsibility that receives the least attention. These relationships ideally are externally focused, for example, with state Medicaid directors, the governor, key health care legislators and influential lobbying groups. Some of the roles and responsibilities of the board chair are also those of the health plan CEO and they can be shared or delegated to the CEO, but this requires support from the board. Much of this depends on the structure of your organization, as larger national health plan companies may have board chairs located out-of-state or the board chair is also the CEO.

The critical point is to be aware of the relationships that need attention and clarity around who owns it (i.e., someone on the board, the CEO or another executive). Some companies assign these external relationship duties to government relations personnel, which is fine but this should be complementary and supplemental to the strategic vision of relationship cultivation by senior leaders such as the board chair and/or CEO. What you are seeking is a mutually trustworthy relationship with state officials. Building that trust takes time and effort and meeting face-to-face when possible. It means meeting with state leaders (Medicaid agency directors as well as governor's office, key health care legislators, etc.) and finding out their needs, goals and concerns. And then following-up with any inquiries posed to you by state leaders. Creating and sustaining relationships will be one of the most important and difficult of all board and CEO responsibilities. It takes time, focus, deliberation and perseverance. Chapters 4 and 5 explore deeper into who else in your health plan owns nurturing relationships with state officials. Reality is, some state officials will not be interested in meeting with you any more than is necessary or not interested in cultivating a partnership that mutually addresses the needs of that state's Medicaid beneficiaries. Some states look at all of this as strictly a contractual arrangement, their role as simply a regulator, and their limits and boundaries need to be respected.

Hiring the Best Leaders

One of the board's most critical roles is hiring the chief executive officer and ensuring appropriate leadership throughout the health plan, especially at the C-level (i.e., chief operating officer, chief medical officer, chief financial officer, etc.). An important attribute for hiring health plan chief executives is Medicaid managed care experience. I have seen CEO's who provided outstanding organizational leadership without a strong Medicaid background, though it has been rare and the organization was already strategically and operationally strong. If the health plan is struggling—either because of operational performance issues, deteriorating state relationships, or severe financial challenges—it does make a difference to hire someone with strong leadership skills and Medicaid managed care experience. The intricacies and complexity of Medicaid managed care and the witnessing of faltering health plans hiring non-Medicaid leaders has convinced me of the importance of relevant experience. Nevertheless, I have witnessed experienced, as well as inexperienced, CEO's fail at a key skill: managing the state relationship and failing to understand the state contractual requirements.

A familiar theme throughout this book is for your leaders to know and understand your state contract. And this goes for all levels of management. A common symptom I found in failing health plans in need of a turnaround, or in mid-phase of an attempted turnaround, was the lack of understanding of contractual requirements virtually at every level of the organization and sometimes no one even knew where to find the contract. You must ensure operational, financial, legal, medical and all other department leaders know and understand the contract. And that they possess a working knowledge of the state's Medicaid agency and the importance of establishing relationships with its leaders and guiding their health plan leaders to develop relationships with their state counterparts. You are striving for relationships that spread over the breadth and depth of the Medicaid agency. This is not just a one-person show in which the health plan CEO and the agency's director meet regularly, but one in which multi-levels of the health plan regularly interact with multi-levels at the agency, strengthening the overall fabric of the relationships. There is more on this in Chapter 5.

Other leadership qualities for the CEO (and other C-level personnel as well) can be found in most any book on leadership and management. They'll list things such as visionary, inspirational, externally focused, self-awareness, even humility. A few will tout the importance of understanding the main customer (in this case, it is the state in which you are contracted with); along with the vulnerable individuals for which you are mutually responsible; the providers who you contract with to deliver health care services to these members; and the measure of humble diligence and authenticity necessary to shepherd all these relationships successfully.

Many of the qualities of these leaders fall under the attributes listed in Jim Collins' (2001) best-selling book *Good to Great*. Collins talks about "Level 5 Leadership," a hierarchy of paradoxical executive capabilities which encompasses a mix of personal humility and professional will. It popularized the notion of first getting the "right people on the bus" (and the wrong people off the bus), before setting new directions or visions or strategies. Collins' book is one of the best out there on leadership and management, as evidenced by its years on best sellers lists.

Charles Green, a contributor to *Forbes* magazine, highlights the value of trust in what leaders need, in the modern era, to be successful. He focuses on leaders who are "good at collaboration and the tools of influence […] operate from a clear set of values and principles […] skilled at the art and science of trust" (Green 2012). Green further states that leaders today need authenticity, the ability to nurture relationships and have a level of emotional intelligence.

The right CEO and board strongly influences the culture of the organization and in fact are responsible for creating the atmosphere for an effective and successful culture. The ones that consistently sustain a level of effectiveness and success (i.e., they remain in good standing with their state, have good satisfaction scores with their providers and members, are financially stable, etc.) are the ones that exude *authenticity, humility, integrity and transparency.* These are additional attributes of leaders your organization should strive to recruit from outside your company and groom from within your company.

Authenticity

Authenticity means having a clear understanding of ones strengths, weaknesses and an acceptance of both as well as no airs about yourself as being superior (or inferior) to others.

Humility

I once witnessed a highly compensated health plan corporate executive behave with an attitude of superiority toward key state Medicaid officials. This was during a lucrative RFP process in which the health plan was renewing its multi-year, multi-million dollar contract via a competitive bid process. The health plan turned in an exceptionally poor RFP response and lost their entire contract. The executive was incensed that the state took this action and strutted around proclaiming that he and his colleagues knew more about Medicaid and capitation rates than the state did and how dare they not award his health plan the contract. Of course, such arrogance and hubris is probably what led the organization to turn in such a losing bid in the first place (after this loss, which was characterized by all as humiliating, I was called in to review the RFP response to determine if the state had mis-scored the health plan's response and found it to be the worst RFP document I have ever read). The post-mortem of what happened to this health plan revealed that the state had been communicating their dissatisfaction with them for quite some time and the relationship was not as mutually wonderful as the local CEO had intimated. This experience not only displayed the necessity of humility in ones leaders, but that it extends to not only local leadership, but regional/corporate leadership as well. Humility is being courteous and respectful, in speech as well as in manner. Too often I have seen well-paid health plan executives flaunt their luxury cars, watches or other accouterments in front of their lesser-paid Medicaid counterparts, only causing resentment and envy. Is that what you really want? I'm not advocating hiding or changing who you are necessarily (see authenticity), but be aware that you are mutually representing vulnerable, poor individuals of your state and this is no place to be showing-off one's wealth. Be yourself, but be respectful, humble and use common sense.

Integrity

To me, no attribute is more important than integrity, as it encompasses trust, honesty and adherence to a moral code. These are people who do what they say they are going to do, and if they cannot deliver, they notify you ahead of time. Their word is solid. You never have to guess their intent or worry about betrayals. These are people your state would want to work with, and hiring someone with integrity means they are also authentic, transparent and humble.

Transparency

A dictionary defines transparency as "easy to notice or understand; honest and open, not secretive; free from pretense or deceit; characterized by visibility, accessibility of information especially concerning business practices" (Merriam-Webster 2016). I've yet to come across a state agency that doesn't expect transparency and honesty from their contracted health plans. Most are delighted with a heads-up of potential performance issues, or major provider challenges (e.g., loss of contract, claims miscues, etc.). In most cases, conducting business with transparency helps solidify a level of trust between your health plan and the state, which goes a long way when operational surprises do occur (and it seems they always do). I've heard executives decry they cannot proceed in this manner with their state, for a variety of reasons, but all of them relate back to a lack of trust between the state and the health plan. There may be insurmountable history with your state and maybe your chance of establishing a deep and trustful relationship may not occur until there is turnover of staff at the state, but I encourage you to endeavor toward a trustful relationship, one with leaders who emulate authenticity, humility, integrity and transparency.

If your health plan is in operational trouble and under scrutiny from your state Medicaid agency, then hiring the right leaders becomes even more relevant and important in fostering an improved relationship with your state. When your top candidate for a key leadership position intersects with the state knowing or having confidence in that person, then you have the potential for a win-win situation. An example of this occurred in a health plan that was experiencing critical operational failures and their contract with the state was in jeopardy. Two actions were taken that enhanced the state's faith in the health plan's turnaround efforts: one was the health plan CEO promoted someone the state knew and had confidence in to oversee one of the areas that contributed to the operational difficulties and the other was to bring onto the plan's board of directors an influential local leader, familiar to and admired by the state, who had extensive Medicaid experience. These two actions alone didn't resolve all the issues, but it did give a sense of relief to the state Medicaid agency that the right people had been brought on board, and this provided the health plan a little breathing room in which to continue its turnaround efforts.

Who Should Be on Your Board?

There was a health plan I worked with years ago that was in serious financial and operational trouble and at risk of losing their billion dollar a year state contract. My first few weeks observed that reports were sent to the state (as part of state reporting requirements) that were never reviewed; different reports were sent to a disembodied corporate office department the content of which had little relevance to state reports; and reports of a third nature were sent to this health plan's board of directors. These reports were not reviewed by any health plan executive; they were simply compiled by staff and sent. It perplexed me that so many reports were sent to so many stakeholders and while there was overlap of data and information, there was no attempt to align any of it, provide oversight or even to evaluate what the data was telling anyone. I decided to start with the CEO and asked, "Who is on your board and how often do you meet"? "I don't know" the CEO responded. This was a talented individual, new to the organization but valued by many other executives, who had been tossed into a quagmire. Firing this CEO wasn't the answer in this case. I knew that this particular state valued appropriate oversight and that part of this health plan's turnaround was going to involve demonstrating effective governance. The answer was creating an effective and active board and developing appropriate processes of governance.

Although each state/Medicaid market has locally owned non-profit or for-profit health plans, there are also several large national health care organizations which are varied in their structural attributes. Some local health plans are wholly owned by larger Health Care Organizations (HCO); some of these have separate boards and some do not (i.e., subsidiaries with their own separate board). For those who are structured with a local board, it is imperative that the composition of the board reflect members of the community (including reflecting the demographic composition of your health plan) and comprise a diversity of relevant skills, gender, age, ethnicity and experience in Medicaid as well as in board service. Equally important are the personal attributes mentioned above of authenticity, humility, integrity and transparency. It is critical that trustworthy individuals who are up to the task of board service and committed to your organization's mission be recruited by the board's nominating committee or governance committee. Ex-Medicaid directors and others of influence can help shape and advance your company's goals. It's back to the oft repeated maxim, "Medicaid is local," meaning each state is unique in its demographics, Medicaid program design, and contractual requirements, so it is important that your board reflect this locality in its membership.

Health plans that are part of a larger national corporation may also have board members who are not local but are part of the corporate structure and sit on the local board for alignment with corporate interests. These board members assist with good stewardship of maintaining overall adherence to corporate mission, financial integrity and reputation.

I mentioned earlier about recruiting board members with diverse skills, backgrounds, ethnicity, etc., and one of the most important attributes is influence. One large health plan I was involved with was desperately seeking a turnaround from years of poor service. I recommended they bring on to their board an ex-Medicaid director, who I knew personally, from that state who had a stellar reputation, deep community ties and certainly relevant experience. This person's board membership immediately raised the profile of the health plan and she was instrumental in repairing relationships not only with the state Medicaid agency, but with providers in the community. Her insights into what the state (and providers) were looking for provided much needed influence in changing behavior, actions and ultimately the culture of the organization. The health plan's eventual successful turnaround wasn't solely dependent on this person, but having people on your board with influence with providers, other agencies (including your state Medicaid agency), the community, other stakeholders and the board itself, can make a difference in creating a sustainable organization.

Many boards also recruit community members-at-large and/or health plan members. Some board membership may be dictated by state requirements (e.g., requiring a health plan member) or require an advisory group comprised of community and health plan members. Sometimes these are in addition to your board or part of your board. Either way, including people from the community—members, providers, non-profit agencies or special interest groups—all provide diversity, a healthy perspective and a good mix of experience, skills and influence that help create a board that is not only robust, but effective and successful in advancing your mission and vision.

There are excellent resources available that detail processes for boards to function effectively and provide structure for board standing committees, building a knowledgeable, accountable and skilled board that excels at governance and mission fulfillment. Whether you are for-profit or non-profit, stand-alone or part of a national enterprise, the resources at the end of this book contain information applicable to all.

Summary of Key Points

- Recruit and build an effective, diverse, passionate board of directors; embrace local talent for these positions as well as corporate personnel (if applicable).
- Recruit key leadership for the health plan based on competency, relevant experience, trustworthiness and maturity (including authenticity, humility, integrity, transparency).
- Meet regularly to approve and provide oversight of strategic direction, operations and major financial decisions, ensure compliance with regulations and contract requirements.
- Create effective communications between local and corporate headquarters (applicable to national companies); ensure clarity around escalation and attention to urgent local issues and awareness of potential conflicts of interest.
- Board of directors needs to counsel and support the CEO and support the state in their endeavors.
- Board chair and/or health plan CEO develops sustainable relationships with the community and state Medicaid leaders (and other state department heads) and effectively listens to their concerns.

Chapter 3

Strategic Planning

One of the most important tasks an organization will undertake is the creation and management of an effective strategic plan. Done well, and used as intended, it provides a road map for your organization's goals, objectives and strategies to meet or exceed its mission and vision and in this case, state goals and contractual requirements. I've heard many CEOs groan and complain about the time wasted on developing a strategic plan that "ends up sitting on a shelf collecting dust." I've heard this phrase so often it has become trite and cliche. Certainly not what one desires when it comes to strategic plans. It seems their organizations either didn't understand the value of an effective strategic plan or only created it to meet some board directive or perhaps a state requirement. Some of these CEOs admitted to me that they simply created other business plans to manage their organization and to meet goals and objectives and I always wondered, why do the double work? Why is this an either/or situation? Simply create one plan that meets your needs. There are various reasons why companies end up in these predicaments; some may be due to false understandings of what a strategic plan is or those CEOs experienced bad management of strategic plans in prior organizations. It seems the notion that they had to do one blocked them from embracing it as a useful exercise and a priceless method to achieving success. I am stressing this distaste for strategic planning from CEOs because I hear it so often and I never cease to be amazed at their repugnancy toward it. It doesn't need to be that way. Let's explore why strategic plans are necessary and good and can be a great way for your organization to collaborate with your state in meeting organizational missions and visions and contractual requirements.

What Is an Effective Strategic Plan?

I've been part of the development of numerous strategic plans with for-profit or non-profit healthcare companies, publicly traded or privately owned enterprises, even a church, and the best ones all had the same attributes. They were:

1. Focused on achieving the organizations' mission, vision and values.
2. Aspirational in their goal setting and desires to achieve something great.
3. Mindful of incorporating some aspect of social responsibility.
4. Collaborative in their strategic planning development; a process that was inclusive of board members, senior executives of the health plan, lower level staff and/or community members and was reviewed and approved by these senior leaders and the board.
5. Diligent about regularly monitoring, measuring and if necessary, adjusting the strategic plan to meet changing market needs. The plan never sat on a shelf collecting dust.
   For Medicaid managed care plans, I would add:
6. Incorporate review of external research and factors such as:
   - Your states' Medicaid strategic plan or overall health care vision.
   - Any mission or vision that might be stated in your governor's state of the state address or expressed in some other similar document.
   - Introduce the notion of your health plan and the state Medicaid agency partnering together to solve issues affecting both parties, leaving room for creative, innovative problem-solving (more on this later).

Too often health plans develop their strategic plan with no realization or knowledge of their state's needs or expectations of their contracted Medicaid health plans. The health plan frequently is under regional or national corporate pressure to achieve certain results—and I understand that perspective and the pressure that comes with it. But before budgets are finalized, I encourage you to learn first where your state is at, what are their priorities and needs? The easy and quick response is money. Consider that many states are also facing considerable pressure to stay within budgets and also address numerous issues raised by their legislature and constituents. I believe more can be achieved by working together rather than in silos or against each other as adversaries in the race to the financial bottom line. Keep in mind all you have in common—budgets and the shared responsibility of the betterment of health of Medicaid beneficiaries. Incorporating elements into your strategic plan that meets mutual goals or helps your state meet a strategic goal(s) of their own helps create a trustworthy relationship.

One health plan I assisted had never read their state's five-year strategic plan until I brought it to their attention. In it were standard descriptions of keeping costs down for taxpayers' sake, improving health outcomes for Medicaid populations, etc. But one of the state's six strategic goals was related to their large (and disenfranchised) Native American population and suddenly the CEO's eyes popped open bright and curious about a potential opportunity. The health plan just happened to have a relationship with one of the tribes in that state. Putting together a few ideas of how to make this work for the state quickly got added to the health plan's strategic plan and money was allocated in the budget process. And it wasn't a huge budget change since the resources already existed, but the value it provided for the state—and the surprise that the health plan had read and understood the state's own strategic plan and met with them to discuss—was priceless. Oftentimes, old behavior patterns set in in our meetings with state officials, and their need for Native Americans had never been raised. But it was important to them; they just never saw the health plans as being part of the solution. You, too, have the opportunity to break old behavior patterns and bring ideas and solutions to your state.

So I encourage you to think creatively of how you can help your state achieve the unachievable and make it part of your own strategic plan. Grandiose plans or huge expensive overtures aren't necessarily needed to create lasting state relationships—as many things in life, and as was the case with the aforementioned health plan—it is the collection of small things that add up to something bigger and can make a difference.

Elements of a Strategic Plan

The best strategic plans start with a formal process of examining what is needed for your health plan to move forward and meet its mission. The people involved in this process include your board chair and additional board members as needed, senior leaders of the health plan, other internal staff and external stakeholders (this may include regional and/or corporate individuals). The strategic plan "seeks to align the internal operations with external exigencies in developing strategic goals along with action plans to achieve them" (Wertheimer 2013). As mentioned before, the strategic plan is a framework for meeting your health plan's mission. Before developing your strategic plan, it is important to understand your plan's (and parent organization, if applicable) planning and budget cycles, and align yourself with that so your strategic plan is in good position with fiscal year budgets and state requirements.

There are numerous resources on the market for strategic plans. Just as I earlier shared what the successful ones had in common, they also share the following in their creation (adapted from *The Board Chair Handbook*, 2013):

1. *Reviewing/revising your mission statement*: Regularly reviewing your mission, vision and values statement is a healthy exercise to assess relevancy and whether or not you are addressing the needs of your key stakeholders (i.e., the state, your Medicaid beneficiaries). This review should be done in collaboration with senior leaders and the board and never done in isolation.
2. *Assess internal and external environments*: You'll want a good understanding of what operational challenges you may have vis-a-vis external changes and requirements.
3. *Assess strategic issues*: Use the information gathered in the step above; this is where the discovery that the aforementioned health plan could help the state with Native Americans was key and was incorporated into the plan's goals and objectives.
4. *Develop strategic goals*: Five to seven goals are typically created for a two-to-three or five-to-ten-year strategic plans; they are discussed by the full board and approved via vote for a final set of goals. This is done by senior leaders if no board exists. Create aspirational goals that are measurable.
5. *Create action plans*: Most organizations I worked with took the main strategic goals (usually five to seven goals are outlined for the next five years or so). Each goal contains objectives and strategies to meet those goals. There may be two to three objectives for each goal. And three to five strategies for each objective. These are all compiled into one document from which a standard action plan can be created. It is important that the strategies and objectives are measurable, so you know when they are achieved or on track.

Each goal, objective and strategy has an owner responsible for implementation, along with due dates for expected completion and the status of progress made toward completion. Also, how each will be measured and what resources might be needed to be successful. This is why it is important to know the timing of budgets (including the state's) and other financial considerations so that appropriate funding is available to attain certain objectives within the strategic plan.

6. *Monitor and evaluate the strategic plan*: There's an old saying "plan your work and work your plan" and it certainly applies to your strategic plan. CEOs who chuck it aside and shelve it may occasionally be successful and some do just fine flying by the seat of their pants, but eventually the holes in this approach get bigger and failure ensues. The more successful and long-lasting organizations (and we are striving toward long-lasting and sustainable success) are those that use their strategic plan as a dynamic and living document and their state counterpart as a trustworthy partner in the process. Furthermore, meet with your state to review progress and challenges on your strategic plan (as applicable), especially any goals that were developed as a result of state meetings or are of great interest to your state. Demonstrate to them that you have their interests in mind and seek to advance the state's own goals and objectives in addition to your own.

Executing Strategic Plans

Once a strategic plan is created and fully fleshed out with assigned accountability and responsibility, due dates and agreed-upon measures, it is imperative to use and review the plan throughout the work year. Meet with your board, C-suite of leaders and your staff to regularly review status and any necessary changes to your strategic plan, and:

■ See this as a way to augment your relationships with your health plan leaders and staff.
■ Involve them in the process and hold them accountable for their deliverables.
■ Challenge your staff to seek solutions or recommendations to areas that are difficult to achieve.
■ Ensure your leaders and staff have the resources to achieve their respective areas of responsibility.
■ Be willing to adjust goals and/or resources as a changing market may require.

I recommend to even be willing to meet with your state Medicaid director or other agency managers, to discuss those areas that overlap or represent mutual goals between the state and your health plan. If both of you are struggling to achieve the same goals, are other health plans in the same market also struggling? Is there another way to tackle this issue? Brainstorming creative solutions with your state counterparts can be a great way to strengthen relationships as well as finding ways to solve health issues faced by your state's Medicaid population.

Effective execution of your plan means reviewing the actual plan on a regular basis with health plan leaders and staff. This requires creating the discipline of review such as weekly updates conducted by staff and managers, monthly reviews by senior health plans leaders (e.g., C-level executives) and quarterly updates with your board (as applicable). Effective meetings start with a specific purpose and a desired outcome (e.g., review of the strategic plan goal number two, assessing any changes to its timeline or resources required); this is conducted with the personnel responsible for delivering on this goal, reporting on its progress and challenges, and bringing recommendations for any necessary alterations. These regular review meetings become essential as too many things can happen during the course of a business fiscal year: budget crises at the health plan or at the state level that impacts health plan financials; operational or compliance issues; or any other health plan hiccup that can change the direction and execution of your strategic plan.

Two examples of well-done strategic plans remain in my memory. One was for a large, for-profit health plan in which a spreadsheet was used to capture the main goals, objectives, strategies, persons responsible, due dates, status (i.e., on track or not). This document was prefaced with the organization's mission and vision and served as a solid foundation to what followed. Senior executives reported on their respective portions at each executive meeting. Sometimes the time allotted to the strategic plan was consumed by the needs of one area. Other times, all executives had a chance to report on status and any actions needed if their goal was behind schedule. The other organization was smaller, non-profit but had a similar action plan in terms of structure. Their's was compiled into a beautiful handbook that was also prefaced with the organization's mission, vision and values. The senior leaders and staff of this organization owned implementing the plan and reported progress to the board several times a year.

The first organization had a more formal reporting schedule and a more robust monitoring process (perhaps due to its size and for-profit designation). The second organization was less formal and less aggressive in its regular review of their strategic plan, but both were successful in furthering their mission, accomplishing their goals and meeting financial targets and other aspirations. Both succeeded in large part because they created well-structured strategic plans, implemented them, monitored and evaluated and made adjustments as needed as time went on. My involvement with the two organizations was enormously pleasant—the senior executive meetings were full of good discussion with creative ideas and decisions made to address issues.

Summary of Key Points

- Conduct strategic planning in concert with your state; be aware of their goals and objectives and discuss with your state as applicable.
- Aspire to achieve great things and create goals that inspire you, your staff and your state.
- Align mutual goals and help your state achieve their's as appropriate.
- Execute your strategic plan with regular review meetings with staff, health plan executives and board review; use these opportunities to additionally strengthen relationships with involved parties.
- Monitor and evaluate your strategic plan regularly and adjust as necessary to meet market demands or resource/financial changes.
- Share progress and challenges with state partner and actions taken to address shortfalls.

CREATING AND SUSTAINING RELATIONSHIPS

II

Chapter 4

Integrating for Success

In this section, I provide a high-level view of four important organizational areas that must be integrated and coordinated in the effort to successfully meet contractual requirements and sustain state relationships. Previous chapters laid the groundwork for the infrastructure I believe is necessary to deliver on contractual requirements, a necessary step in developing and sustaining state relationships. This and the following chapters seek to explain how relationships are integral not only to your external constituents (e.g., your state Medicaid agency, other state agencies, providers, community associations) but also internally with your employees. What follows are ideas, as well as stories, of what has worked well in organizations I have been involved with, along with what hasn't worked well, and the lessons learned from that experience.

Provider Relationships

Medicaid managed care companies contract with various provider groups under a variety of financial mechanisms to serve the medical and/or mental health needs of their enrolled members. Frequently, there are standards set by states on the coverage the provider network must reach. For example, certain geographic regions must have a minimal number (or an explicit number set by the state) of PCPs, specialists, hospitals, dentists, etc. These are generally specified in the contract. These standards are important so that Medicaid beneficiaries have access to necessary health care services. I have seen cases in which the standard cannot be met, such as a state requiring a certain provider specialty in a rural area in which no such provider exists, but such difficulties in meeting a standard open the possibilities of creating something innovative. For example, some Medicaid health plans develop telemedicine opportunities to meet rural health care needs or provide transportation to more urban areas in which a specialist practices. There are, however, health plans which don't recognize what these minimum network standards are. For some, the only time they look at the standards are when an audit or RFP is imminent, or the state has slapped a penalty or sanction on the health plan for failure to meet standards. It's not the best way to conduct business and leaves the state with a bad impression of you and your company. If your provider network is lacking, chances are your members are complaining or your medical services team is frustrated with increased out-of-network utilization.

The point is, read and understand your state contract as it relates to provider coverage and mobilize the staff needed to create that provider network. This isn't a simple process as a lot of human resources and money can be involved, but you essentially have no health plan without a provider network. It is also important to include other viewpoints from your health plan staff in contracting or re-contracting your network. Three main areas to include are: quality, medical services and finance. Your provider contracting team needs to know of any quality issues through dialogue with their staff and review of their reports, which may include—information the state has gathered, review of medical records, accreditation materials, certifications, etc. The managed care model assumes you are contracting with a select group of providers who meet a higher standard than providers at large and are expected to be certified in their specialty, licensed in good standing with state medical review boards, the Joint Commission and other review agencies for hospitals. It is incumbent upon you and your provider staff to coordinate with the quality department in your contracting efforts.

In a similar vein, the same holds true with your medical services team. Meeting with your chief medical officer (CMO) and supporting leaders and staff can help determine which providers over or under-utilize medical services; claims reviews and medical office reviews to determine appropriate vaccines and preventative services; in-hospital medical reviews can assist in determining appropriate lengths of stay, outcomes on various hospitalization diagnoses and more. Your provider services department should also be conducting their own research and compiling accessibility and availability data, provider satisfaction survey information, member satisfaction survey information (as it relates to your provider network and the services coordinated by the health plan) and finance input on feasible ranges for capitated and fee-for-service contracts along with past financial performance.

You'll want to have leverage at the negotiating table, so compile the above information and bring it along to contracting discussions. Many plans bring their CMO for providers who are key to your overall network but are sometimes challenging at the contract table. The CMO's overall role at the health plan and understanding of quality, provider and medical services may be critical to a signed and mutually acceptable contract. Good contracts between the health plan and its provider network incorporate all the above elements as well as instill performance expectations and incentives for desired results. This latter point is especially important. Expected performance metrics should be part of your provider contract in order to ensure they meet state contractual requirements and these metrics need to be regularly monitored, evaluated and shared with the provider. Hold them accountable for the services they are providing your members just as they will be holding you accountable to pay timely on their claims.

These steps are fundamental to creating a provider network that serves your members well and meets state contractual requirements. But it is more than just forming the network and checking off boxes of state requirements; it is also gathering important external data points that inform you of how well you are doing with your network and services. Here is a list, compiled from several health plans, of what they did to create a superior provider network and provider services, continuously asking themselves "how do we keep our providers happy?":

■ *Established relationships with influential provider associations/societies*: This varies with states; it may be your local medical society or other similar organizations. Usually this level of relationship is owned or managed by the CEO or board chair (or other board member), sometimes government relations staff leader, depending on how your company is organized. As an example, one health plan I worked with had an organization in their state that represented hospitals and other healthcare organizations which was very influential with state legislators and state agencies. A relationship with them was essential, even if the health plan and this organization didn't always see eye-to-eye; it was critical that they meet regularly and openly discussed their needs, expectations and visions. This particular organization conducted annual surveys of providers' satisfaction with area health plans (in the Medicaid, Medicare and commercial industry); these survey results were widely distributed. Reviewing these results and addressing the less-than-satisfied areas contributed to much higher scores in future surveys, and resulted in the state Medicaid agency in viewing this health plan in a more favorable light.

■ *Listened to provider complaints*: Quite often a health plan in trouble is measured by the volume of provider complaints that bypass the plan (usually due to lack of responses from the plan) and go directly to the state, sometimes to the director and in severe cases, to the state's governor. A priority is to lessen this noise by addressing the key issues—usually it is claims payment, or turnaround times on appeals. Make sure these are addressed along with meeting with those providers to diffuse their anger and frustration with you. This may all seem rather elementary, but you would be surprised at how often health plans have not bothered to reach out to these providers or to take their concerns seriously and address long-standing claims problems. Pay the claims and quiet the noise, or you will never get to the point of establishing a trustworthy relationship.

■ *Regularly surveyed their provider network*: These results were reviewed and action plans were created to address the issues and the action plans and progress made was shared with the state. Many states in fact require annual provider surveys, but few health plans follow through and do something with the results. Most health plans ask their provider networks standard questions on satisfaction with claims payments, appeals, ease of reaching their provider representative or health plan claims department, etc. Today, most health plans solicit responses via the Internet or post on their provider portal to make it easy for the provider network to respond. The key is, go the extra mile, review the survey results and address your provider's concerns as revealed in the survey.

■ *Excelled at provider training*: I have heard providers complain that they miss the personal touch of health plan provider services staff personally visiting the offices for training. If you have the provider services representatives who can visit numerous offices for training, then do so. But many resort to online computer-based-training (CBT) modules, supplemented with group trainings, one-on-one follow-up visits, booklets, websites and provider portals with additional information, etc. And to be fair, some provider offices prefer the CBT as they can schedule it into their work day more easily. Overall, you want to make it easy for your providers to do business with you. Ensure that your training includes all aspects of how to reach your organization, ask for help, get issues resolved and how to escalate an issue appropriately.

▪ *Continuously trained all employees*: Employees with provider touchpoints (e.g., call center staff, and personnel in provider services, claims, contracting) were continuously educated in the company's mission, vision and values, and coached on the messages to be communicated to the providers. This was accomplished through CBT, classroom group training sessions, one-on-one coaching and importantly, emulated and modeled by health plan leadership (i.e., practicing what you preach). Many health plans employ a customer service approach mentality that has been successful in other industries (banking, retail, veterinary services and more).

▪ *Reviewed member satisfaction survey results*: High-functioning health plans took provider-related questions from member surveys and reviewed them for any insights or actions that could be taken (this means your member satisfaction survey must have provider relevant questions). Good member surveys ask questions about availability and access to your provider network, how they are treated in the office (or hospital). Ask members what providers they wish were in your network—you may be surprised by this win-win if the provider turns out to be a good partner for you.

▪ *Creative and innovative in meeting state needs*: For example, provider shortages are not uncommon, especially in rural areas, and programs like telemedicine, traveling medical vans, nurse practitioners/physician assistants and other physician extenders can be employed. Work with any local medical schools to assist or coordinate with other health plans or providers to apply for grants that address provider shortages.

▪ *Recruited influential physicians to the board of directors:* In some organizations, representatives of influential provider groups (if physicians were unable) were appointed to governing boards, giving those providers/representatives insight to issues the health plan faces and a voice in ideas and decisions made by the board. The transparency and openness of the board paved the way for a more trusting relationship among provider groups and with those these physicians interacted with.

▪ *Explored partnering with provider groups*: They sought groups that could potentially work together to address specific medical needs of your community or raised by the state. Providers can be your partner, too. I have worked with health plans that successfully partnered with different providers and together applied for grants that addressed unique needs of their community, such as creating programs to address autism, or partnered on mobile mammography or vaccinations (especially helpful in rural areas).

The repeating themes are: (1) gathering data and turning it into meaningful information; reviewing that information in context of past and/or desired performance, and taking action to narrow any gaps between actual and desired performance; and (2) don't gather and address data/information in a vacuum, but meet with your providers regularly, and share the data and desired outcomes. Meet with your state counterparts and again share the data and expected outcomes. Developing trust with others takes time and is dependent on the small steps of creating a relationship, that is, meeting preferably face-to-face but even by phone, to establish expectations and the desire to work together in reaching mutual goals. The information should also be shared with your board for their input, oversight and direction. Demonstrate to the state that you have checks and balances in your processes and involve leaders across various internal and external environments to develop and emulate a governance process that yields positive results.

Member Relationships

One of the most rewarding aspects of working in Medicaid, and Medicaid managed care in particular, is the relationships and encounters with those entrusted to us by the state for their health and well-being needs. It is a unique arrangement in which the Medicaid health plan and the state Medicaid agency are accountable stewards for our nation's most vulnerable and disenfranchised individuals.

A good health plan works hard at member retention, and they achieve this through actively addressing any fixable issues identified in satisfaction surveys; conducting member events in the field and listening to feedback from members who are able to attend; listening to state representatives who frequently advocate for health plan interventions on behalf of members; and listening to providers who are the ones who most frequently interact with your members and quite often have good suggestions on how to create or improve relationships and member satisfaction. Keeping these lines of communication open and transparent will generally create opportunities for improvements (OFIs). In addition, many health plans participate with various advocacy groups in order to understand the perspective and needs of specialty populations (see community relationship section). Furthermore, many members' only interaction with a health plan happens on the phone when they call member services; this provides a unique and key opportunity to do a point of service survey (i.e., did we answer your questions to your satisfaction? Are you satisfied with XYZ Health Plan?).

Creating and sustaining positive relationships with your Medicaid members can be tricky because they can so easily drop off your enrollment roster or just as easily be added-on via auto-enrollment. Annual (or more frequently) member satisfaction surveys are common and generally required by state Medicaid contracts. As important as these instruments are, they can be a distant and detached relationship with your member. Nevertheless, they must be done, reviewed by member services staff and others, in addition to leadership, to address any misses with expectations. Here are additional thoughts to establish closer relationships with your members in the quest to keep them happy:

- *Train member call center staff:* And train them adequately enough and, as mentioned above, consider one minute survey questions at the phone call point of entry to gauge member satisfaction instantly. It can be a simple, "were you satisfied with this call?"
- *Continuously train all employees*: Similar to provider services, employees with member touchpoints (e.g., call center staff, member services personnel, care coordinators, member appeals, outreach, case managers) need to be trained in your mission, vision and values and coach your staff on the messages to be communicated to your members. Try employing a customer service approach that has been successful in other industries.
- *Listen to your providers*: Your provider network most likely has more frequent interactions with your members (and hears their concerns) and could provide you with ideas for improvement, especially since member surveys are typically not filled out by any majority. Some examples may include availability of transportation to provider offices, ease of getting prescriptions filled, ability to get through to member services, etc.
- *Identify key community organizations*: Develop relationships with those that advocate for your members and develop relationships with them, for example, Children's Alliance, autism groups, mental health advocates, developmentally disabled groups, homeless centers, etc. (See the community section for more detail.)

■ *Initiate mobile van services or other creative outreach methods*: Mobile van services are not a new idea, but they have been quite successful in rural and urban areas to address the frequent issue of accessibility to services (such as transportation difficulties) as well as addressing outreach to members. Mobile vans have been used for mammography, vaccines, weight and blood pressure checks, assisting with provider appointments and more.

■ *Consider a member advisory committee*: These can be implemented whether or not your state requires it. Or, adding a member or previous Medicaid beneficiary to your board. Their insights and experiences may be helpful in your strategic planning, operational assessments and services provided.

Community and Other External Relationships

One health plan I was involved with was criticized by its state Medicaid agency for not being committed to the state and not caring about the community in which it operated. It was a stinging indictment of our lack of community awareness and ties. Upon further review, their statement, unfortunately, was true and followed years of little health plan (and corporate) support for any community involvement or organizational support related to members. Very few people at the plan even seemed to be aware that this might be important to the state. The state viewed us as bloodless corporate robots, going through the motions to collect a paycheck. We had a lot of work to do to turnaround the state officials' impression of us.

One of the first steps was understanding the demographics of the members we served. If state Medicaid demographic data is difficult to come by, census data by member zip code can be used as a proxy. This particular health plan happened to be involved with the local National Urban League organization (a non-profit focusing on civil rights of African-Americans and others), which enjoyed a great relationship that we all recognized needed to be sustained. But the plan was located in the Southwestern United States; its Medicaid population (and the state's) was only 5% Black and nearly 40% Hispanic. There was minimal interaction with any of the various Hispanic organizations in the state. There were no interactions with organizations that supported children or assisted women—the majority of enrollees in the Nation's Medicaid program. We successfully changed this dynamic by creating new relationships. Here are some of the actions we took:

■ Identified key demographic organizations (usually non-profit) that represent your member constituents and advocate for them, like children's alliances, mental health organizations, various disease associations (e.g., autism, developmentally disabled), Hispanic, Black, Asian, Native American or other race/ethnic groups served by your health plan/state Medicaid program to understand their unique needs and perspectives. Created programs to address and collaborate with others to assist these groups. Again, relationship owners at this level are typically board members, the CEO, or government relations leaders or other senior executives at your health plan.

■ Encouraged community involvement with your staff. We found in this particular health plan that many staff regularly volunteered an incredible number of hours at various places in the state, but nothing was ever coordinated to make more of an impact on any one organization. Employees were asked about organizations of interest vis-a-vis organizations with needs that assisted Medicaid beneficiaries or potential beneficiaries—such as homeless shelters, food banks and kitchens, reading programs for children, etc. There are always non-profits in common between the two and efforts were made to promote and advertise the need to employees and to coordinate the volunteerism. This was not mandated or required; it was all free choice but a coordinated effort has a better chance of impact on the people served by the organization. The employees at this plan enjoyed volunteering together at these various organizations where their strength in numbers could make a greater difference.

■ In addition to actual community involvement, the plan also began to share with the state a more human side of the health plan. That is, revealing that many of the plan's leaders and staff had lived in the state for decades, raised their children, attended local churches, paid taxes and buried loved ones. Demonstrating a commitment to the state beyond just the Medicaid contract took time. It also required the commitment to meet state contractual requirements; the failure to do so is what got the health plan into trouble in the first place.

This approach worked well enough to experience some positive side benefits from establishing tight community relationships. When tough times fell upon one health plan, and they were struggling with their state Medicaid agency relationship, community organizations stood up and supported the leaders of the health plan, softening the state's stance against them and provided them with more time to right the ship and get things back on track at the plan. Another health plan was assisted by local advocacy groups in its rural areas, supported by these groups for outreach to difficult populations.

It's all back to "Medicaid is local." You will want to build strong local relationships with community organizations, community leaders, inviting community officials to join your board, volunteering at local community events and finding or creating opportunities to be involved in your local area.

Sub-contractors is another external relationship that requires attention and due diligence. Some health plans subcontract out a variety of services, such as claims services, call centers, enrollment, mailings (member benefit information, outreach activities) and more. Monitoring their activities is as important as monitoring your own. You are still responsible for ensuring your sub-contractors performance meets state contractual requirements. Make sure your contract with these sub-contractors contains language that spells out what performance metrics they must meet and the consequences of not meeting them. Even if the contract is an internal one within a large corporation. Not having any recourse or repercussions for poor performance can be problematic with your state if you are not able to meet their expectations.

In addition, states are looking for more local alignment and employment of local vendors for operational activities such as claims, call centers, or transportation. There is more state emphasis nowadays on health plans contracting with women or minority-owned/managed vendors. These subcontracted vendors need to be held accountable as mentioned above, via effective contracts and oversight. The accountability is a two-way street: be sure to pay them timely, meet with them regularly and share performance metrics and ensure that any missteps are communicated and addressed completely.

Employee Relationships

Achieving positive results operationally and financially, along with high employee satisfaction and low employee turnover, has a greater chance of success when employees are engaged and committed to your mission and the mission of your state.

Creating a cultural environment that breeds success takes time and effort. But the effort is well worth it if it results in positive outcomes for the health plan, Medicaid members and other stakeholders. One cultural habit that I advocate are regular cross-functional department meetings, which over time provides the benefit of what I call interconnectedness. I once heard an executive lament about his poor-functioning team that they "have siblings, but no family." What he meant was that there was little to no concern (or interest) about the impact one department's actions could have on another; or even an understanding of what another department's responsibilities could have on their own or its impact on the state contractual requirements and state relationship. One example involved a provider contracting staff who were bragging about their renewal of a contract with a large provider group, who had been difficult to re-negotiate with. They felt victorious and announced their success at an informal meeting of staff celebrating someone's birthday. In attendance were the medical staff (including the CMO) who sat in disbelief. This was a provider group who were a thorn in their side with questionable quality outcomes, continuous over-utilization, and difficult for medical and quality staff to work with. The medical team was not happy that this provider group had been re-signed without their input into the process. But there was no venue for that discussion to take place. There was no precedent for those kind of conversations.

Once those venues were created—via regular cross-functional department meetings with clear agendas—this type of episode decreased. The meetings were implemented to provide clear expectations of sharing vital information and engaging in discussions that helped each department to be successful. Sometimes the meetings were just informational—contracting staff announcing who they were entering negotiations with—and other staff (medical, quality, finance) could weigh-in with comments. The positive outcomes from this subtle shift in approach took time to achieve, but the results from increased communications, meaningful inter-departmental meetings and sharing of data was palpable.

There are some key structural components necessary for building solid employee relationships:

■ *Recruit and hire diverse staff*: Recruit those who are reflective of the population you serve. This can be hard to accomplish unless you specifically recruit from organizations that support this notion, such as local community colleges or universities that have programs to graduate diverse students and provide assistance in job searches. These institutions can be great pipelines of future employees. Or collaborate with local Hispanic Chambers of Commerce, the Urban League and other organizations that represent diverse race, ethnic and religious individuals. Selecting, orienting, training, mentoring and further developing your employees takes a robust and comprehensive human resource and development program. Those health plans that do this consistently and with purpose are generally more successful than those that don't.

■ *Train and orient your employees*: This is especially true regarding your state contract, as constantly stressed in this book. Your staff need to be educated on topics like state regulations, quality standards, an overview of Medicaid, confidentiality, compliance, etc. Most states require evidence of initial (for new employees) as well as ongoing/annual training. As mentioned before, training on your state contract is a must, especially managers and senior leaders. All employees should receive an initial orientation (to your company, such as mission, vision, values, employee expectations in addition to state required education) and ongoing training for compliance refreshers and updates. Also helpful, as previously mentioned, is training on a state/Medicaid tailored customer service/state relationship. Focus your training on those who interact first with your members (e.g., call center staff); train them on appropriate messaging and timeliness on follow-up.

■ *Mentor employees*: Some organizations have formal mentoring programs for their employees, partnering them up with senior leaders throughout the enterprise, even if they are located in another state. One idea I heard discussed was mentoring and orienting between a Medicaid health plan and the state Medicaid agency, allowing employees from each organization to learn more about the other. Strict confidentiality would need to be enforced, but the notion of understanding how life is on the other side can be enlightening and helpful.

■ *Communicate*: Did you ever work for an organization in which people mysteriously disappeared as if they just evaporated and were never actually employed there? Or the opposite, when a new employee suddenly shows up and is in charge of a major project or department and no one knows who it is? Neither change came with any communication about the impending personnel change, leaving employees scratching their heads and harrumphing about the lack of information, transparency or announcement of job openings, etc. I always marveled at the number of times this would happen at companies and then senior management wondered why employee morale was low. Nothing works better than good old-fashioned communication. It doesn't have to be complicated, in fact, the simpler the better; the key is to do it and do it consistently, honestly and with purpose. New employees should be introduced to their department, and depending on the level of authority, company-wide. Likewise, inform staff of departing employees. Again, the distribution of such notices depends on their level of authority, that is, the more senior the employee, the more it should be communicated to all staff. Even if this departure is not by the employee's choice, the fact that they are no longer with your company should be shared; you don't have to say why but be respectful and communicate what you can say. The purpose behind these kind of communications is to build trust with your employees and a foundation of expectations that you will share appropriate information with them. Most employees have a desire to be in the know. Not knowing and not understanding fuels rumors and discontent. Two large (greater than 300,000 members) health plans I worked with employed several communication strategies to keep their employees informed. These included:

- *Regular staff meetings:* Organized and structured to inform employees (of business changes, budget changes, etc.), celebrate achievements, highlight new projects or completion of projects, welcome new employees, celebrate birthdays, etc.
- *Informational emails*: One health plan used this strategy as a weekly communique to dampen the rampant rumor-mill occurring during a very difficult period at the health plan. Once order was restored within senior management ranks, the weekly emails decreased in frequency (and in need, based on employee feedback).
- *Newsletters*: Newsletters can be used instead of emails, but typically newsletters are used to highlight employee activities and other interests and generally are not issued as frequently as emails.
- *Informal lunch meetings with executives and staff*: This provides a more intimate atmosphere in which the CEO or other executives (even board members) could really learn what employees were thinking and worried about, or even hear some good ideas.

Good communications are also needed with your state partner regarding employee departures and arrivals. Be sure to adhere to state contractually mandated notifications of key personnel changes and have at the ready a back-up plan to cover that person's responsibilities if a permanent replacement is not immediately available.

■ *Good human capital structure*: I'm an advocate of the structure-process-outcome model described in Chapter 5. Applied to human capital, this means having appropriate job descriptions and job expectations, confidentiality policies, performance evaluations, competitive pay, standard human resource policy and procedures, appropriate due process for employees who do not meet expectations, etc. And then the appropriate processes to carry out these activities. This also includes regular satisfaction surveys. This is a common method to understand what your employees are thinking and feeling about your organization, but too many companies ignore the results or fail to take action to address areas in need of improvement. I've seen some companies shine by taking the responses seriously, forming small employee workgroups to address issues and then communicate, communicate, communicate the changes and improvements to all employees. Don't bother doing an employee satisfaction survey if you are not committed to sharing the results and taking action on shortcomings and communicating status on those actions.

■ *Have fun*: I worked with one health plan executive during a grueling turnaround effort who made a point to his employees to have fun. There certainly was a lot of work to be done to turn this health plan around and the stress involved was high. This executive made sure there were employee committees responsible for planning fun activities (this ranged from simple potlucks, to group volunteering events to simple bowling parties). There was fun incorporated into the office work itself, including showing up for work dressed in costume for Halloween, or making a regular department meeting an occasional potluck meal and sharing favorite recipes. There were various ways, maybe not everyday, but nearly every week to help make it fun for people to do their work and accomplish big goals together. When achieved, these milestones were celebrated (more fun) and the staff involved were thanked and recognized.

■ *Accountability and responsibility*: Recruiting and hiring the right people means placing them in the right positions, something Jim Collins (2001) referred to as getting the "right people on the bus, the right people in the right seats, and the wrong people off the bus." I would add that you then hold those right people accountable for their actions and what they are hired to do. Make it clear to them what their responsibilities are and what expectations are (e.g., provide clear and concise job descriptions, appropriate training and mentoring). As mentioned above, ensure your human capital structural pieces are in place so employees are treated fairly, timely and competently. Two different health plan examples come to mind with accountability and responsibility. One was a large health plan in the East in which upon my arrival, I found to be a jumble of earnest, hard-working individuals with no discernible organizational structure, no clear lines of responsibility and a state agency which was so frustrated with the lack of action and years of persistently poor performance, it had given up calling the local office and went straight to corporate in another state. No one really knew what someone else was responsible for and there was a complete lack of accountability, which led to nothing getting improved since no one really owned the issue (it doesn't matter what the issue was—claims, medical services, compliance—they were all disorganized and poorly functioning). For example, although someone might have the title of provider services director, they had nothing to do with the provider call center, provider training or provider contracting. And they weren't quite sure who did those things. This had the effect of all sorts of leaders and managers who were excellent, but in the wrong "seats" and therefore not able to perform at their peak level. This was old-fashioned organizational chaos caused by structural collapse and management incompetence, in addition to a lack of appropriate oversight by its governing body (i.e., which could be a board of directors or corporate office or both). It took a new CEO (the old one was another example of the Peter Principle, see below) and a welcomed re-organization to get "like types" together and coordinated under capable leadership. Job descriptions were dusted off (not needing that much updating, they just needed to be used as a starting-point and guideline), many employee meetings were conducted to get the "right people, right seat, right bus" mentality to fruition. It took time, but it was finally accomplished with great strides made in improving the state relationship, which, once metrics the state had been complaining about for years started to improve, it opened the door for health plan staff to reignite long-stagnant professional relationships with their state counterparts.

At the opposite end of the country was an equally large health plan, in deep trouble with their state for many of the same reasons as mentioned previously (although they were far better organized). The employee issue here was not having the right people in the right seat. The CEO of this health plan was a good leader but one who chose his staff based on loyalty and past relationships, not necessarily for competency in the position they were hired into. This led to a widespread case of the Peter Principle—in which selection of a candidate for a position is based on the candidate's performance in their current role, rather than on abilities relevant to the intended role; "people are promoted to their level of incompetence" (Goleman 2000). Even good CEOs need to have good leaders and managers around them, so if the right position (or "seat") could not be found for many of this CEO's key leaders, they had to be let go.

It is also essential that the organizational structure serves the needs of your state customer and Medicaid members. That is, someone is your CMO, directors over claims, member services, provider services, medical services, quality, etc. You want to avoid the one health plan described previously in which it wasn't clear who was responsible for what—to the state and quite frankly, to any casual observer. A common symptom I found in nearly every struggling, failing health plan were unclear responsibilities, confusing organizational structure and no clear accountability.

Summary of Key Points

- Regularly measure the satisfaction of your providers, members, and employees; put action plans in place and regularly evaluate progress.
- Cultivate and sustain external relationships with key providers, community organizations, industry associations, advocacy organizations and other influential people and groups. Involve the board, C-level in the relationship building and maintenance.
- Consider local providers, community influencers, member advocates to be on your governing board.
- Hold providers and any sub-contractors accountable for their contractual obligations and ensure performance metrics are outlined, measured and evaluated regularly.
- Seek local women or minority-owned/-managed vendors for any sub-contractual work.
- Recruit and hire diverse staff, provide a rigorous orientation and encourage participation in community volunteer efforts; promote fun along with a culture of accountability and responsibility.

- Integrate employee leaders from key departments to facilitate communication of critical importance regarding provider services, member services, compliance, quality, medical services and finance, etc.
- Make educating and training of your employees (and providers) part of your "culture of discipline." Ensure your employees understand state and other contractual requirements, especially for their departments.
- Foster innovation and creativity, especially with your employees, to solve operational and other challenges.
- Maintain employee accountability with clear job descriptions, training, evaluation and feedback.

Chapter 5

Creating Lasting State Relationships

Why do relationships matter? Is it to form a togetherness that accomplishes more than can be done alone, by ourselves? Is it to develop a sense of community among our co-workers and external stakeholders? Is it to develop mutual trust in a working environment? Perhaps it is a bit of all the above.

Relationships tie to our sense of purpose and mission fulfillment, as described in Chapter 1. This notion of cultivating relationships is not just a concept and it's not just going to happen. It takes deliberate planning, commitment and action, and even some metrics to determine whether you've gotten to where you want (or need) to be. Creating trustful partnerships, either with your board, staff or your state Medicaid agency, takes time and energy. You need to start with the desire to have a sustainable relationship with your stakeholders (in this case, particularly with your Medicaid agency) and choosing to have it. And then like so many other goals in this book, it's developing a plan to meet the objective of creating lasting relationships. This is a detailed approach that gets down to the individual levels in your organization (including yourself) and individuals in your community (including the Medicaid agency). You can meet with your team and have a discussion around what would a lasting relationship (with your state agency/agencies) look like and how do we get there? Perhaps you are struggling with finances and find a relationship with the state is strained due to sub-optimal rates. Your team might agree that higher reimbursement rates from the state would improve matters. What steps would be necessary to achieve that? Meeting with the governor or governor's office, key health care legislators, state budget director? When do you meet and how often? Who meets with them? Or perhaps there are contractual requirements that are difficult or impossible to achieve and failure to meet these contributes to friction in your state relationship. Now who do you meet with to effectuate change? The state Medicaid director, the head of the department the unmet contractual requirement relates to? Any of these changes or achievements are quantifiable and can be incorporated into measuring your effectiveness at relationship building. What might these metrics look like? You can capture such things as:

- The frequency of meetings with key stakeholders
- Who met with the key stakeholders
- The critical dates to incorporate into planning (e.g., state budget meetings, legislative actions on health care issues, governor's state of the state speech—in which new directives related to Medicaid may be announced)

In addition, you can document agenda topics for the meetings and strategically determine what these need to be over the next several months. Examples include: budget planning, contractual requirements changes, topics of interest to the state as well as your own, issues confronting the Medicaid population and participating health plans (such as transportation, homelessness, increasing no-show rates at physician offices, etc.). Overall, the objective is to develop a systematic pathway to lasting relationships and to think beyond one-year time frames but instead focus on a longer horizon—three to five years out into the future. Another way is to time limit the planning to the length of your contract with the state.

A benefit for ongoing relationships with your state and other external stakeholders is getting your work known in the community. Quite often health plans are making a difference in their community, beyond what they are achieving with their Medicaid members, but few in the state are aware of the health plan's impact and influence. Cultivating and nurturing these external relationships helps to inform stakeholders of your involvement and achievements. Sometimes these endeavors result in creating passionate advocates for your health plan, such as community organizations that provide needed services to the Medicaid population. These advocates can assist with legislative actions to expand Medicaid financial support or to soften a state's actions when things go awry at your health plan, for example, when operational miscues occur like claims mishaps. Forming lasting relationships is not an end game of securing favors for you. There is no end—it is perpetual and ongoing for the life of your contract. The best way to delight your state partner and ensure a mutually satisfying business relationship, is to begin meeting or exceeding your contractual requirements.

Who does the relationship building? This is explored a bit more in this chapter in the sense of roles and responsibilities. Adding to that is the choice of executives and staff who are:

■ Passionate about your mission and that of the state's
■ Committed to sustaining the organization and the relationship through the life of the contract
■ Seeking/desiring to engage the community in the relationship cultivation

In addition, this chapter tackles the tactical steps that can sustain relationships as foundational to the aspirational goes of delighting your state Medicaid agency and creating lasting relationships. Structural components are included as well as strategies that can become part of a health plan's business goals and objectives.

Structuring Lasting Relationships

The basic structural components of my approach to effective leadership of Medicaid managed care is an adoption of Dr. Avedis Donabedian's breakthrough health care quality assessment model. I love this model's three simple components: structure, process and outcome (Donabedian 1980). Applied to Medicaid managed care, Donabedian's model, from a high-level perspective for a health plan, might look something like this:

■ *Structure*: Conceptually, the human, physical and financial resources needed to be a Medicaid managed care contractor; the "what," relatively stable, functions to produce/facilitate care and contractual requirements; influences the care provided.
   For example:
   – Mission, vision and values statements (as described in Chapter 1)

- Management and staff (i.e., adequate staffing) and a passionate board of directors
- Appropriate board governance and oversight policies (as discussed in Chapter 2)
- Policies and procedures for all functional areas of the health plan (developed and maintained by health plan staff)
- Provider contracts, sub-contractors with appropriate performance metrics and other related functional elements (as discussed in Chapter 4)
- Financial means and fiscal organization
- State Medicaid contract and a robust compliance plan
- Organizational structure and processes for meetings, monitoring of activities and evaluation (as discussed in Chapter 4)
- Evaluation processes and procedures
- Medicaid beneficiaries (and policy and procedures for enrollment, onboarding and delivery of services)
- Proper system design and technological hardware and software

■ *Process*: The "how," the implementation of the Structure as defined above; it is using the components of Structure in a meaningful manner in order to achieve the best outcomes.

For example:
- Overall continuity, work flow
- Enrolling Medicaid members, servicing their calls, coordinating their care, conducting outreach, etc.
- Contracting with providers, adjudicating claims, servicing their calls, training their offices
- Orientation of staff and ongoing training (see Chapter 4)
- Conducting compliance evaluations to ensure adherence to state Medicaid contractual requirements
- Creating, reviewing and submitting required reports
- Coordination in departments, between departments; internally and externally
- Teamwork, collaborative approach
- Appropriate sequencing of work flows
- Monitoring, measuring key performance indicators (this includes activities by the board as well as the C-suite)
- Minimizing adverse consequences, prevention of issues (as further defined in this chapter)

- Applying principles of Kaizen (continuous improvement) (see www. Kaizen.com)
■ *Outcome:* The "result," a change that can be attributed to antecedent interventions

  For example:
  - Measurable impact (as defined by the board and/or management, your state or other stakeholders; this can be achieved with using balanced scorecards as guidance)
  - Measurable improvements in satisfaction scores, health improvement (e.g., desired rates for decreasing infant mortality, increasing OB/GYN visits, decreasing diabetic adverse outcomes, decreasing ER visits, increasing PCP visits), provider assessments (e.g., availability, responsiveness, satisfaction scores)
  - Meet claims payment deadlines, appeals deadlines, other contractual requirements
  - Financial stability; meeting or exceeding financial/operational goals
  - State satisfaction with health plan performance
  - Use Kaizen principles: "good processes bring good results" (www. Kaizen.com)

These three components, when all organized and coordinated in a systematic and organizationally holistic manner, set the stage for creating and sustaining a state relationship. You must first have your "ducks in a row" before trying to convince a Medicaid agency that you are a worthy partner, and consistently exceed expectations to become a partner the state can't live without.

This is where all the previous chapters come together to provide the foundation of becoming a trusted state partner in a mutually satisfactory relationship. Will this promise a forever-rosy relationship and professional experience with your state? No. But establishing a healthy and trustworthy relationship, concomitant with effective board and C-suite governance, smooths out the rough roads ahead, which will certainly occur. A claims conversion goes awry, provider noise creates havoc, financial hiccups that cause concern for your state, etc. are bound to occur. A strong, healthy relationship with your state could mean the difference between saving your contract or your own job.

Defining Your Main Customer

I touched on who is your main customer in the introduction: Your Medicaid beneficiaries? Your contracted providers? Or is it the state agency you are contracted with? To repeat, the state Medicaid agency is your main customer. This is not to lessen the value or importance of the Medicaid beneficiaries; it is to advance the importance of the state relationship. I see it ignored far too often, with usually dire results.

Your state Medicaid agency is paying you to deliver the services and coordinate medical care for the individuals the state has entrusted to you and which you share in common—the members themselves. There is a mutual agreement that you will deliver on the contractual requirements and the state will compensate you for these services (whether or not you feel their compensation is enough is immaterial right now). Failure to meet the contractual requirements may lead to sanctions, fines or worse. Your job is to operate your business so the contract requirements are met and you meet internal financial goals. Nothing beyond this is actually required.

So why bother fostering a state relationship? Because invariably, as mentioned previously, things will go wrong and you want to have a solid foundation to fall back on. A solid foundation is built by following the principles espoused in this book, and continuously monitoring that state relationship for OFIs. You as the Medicaid managed care executive have an obligation to ensure health care delivery to your members in collaboration with the state. There are inherent desires, on both parties, to actually achieve improved health outcomes, high satisfaction scores (for both members and providers), and partnering with your state advances those notions more readily (and these ideals can be spelled out in mission, vision and values statements). In addition, collaborating with your state agency and understanding their constraints and challenges (state budget cutbacks, anti-Medicaid legislatures, etc.) helps open the door to a more long-lasting, supportive relationship.

There are many issues that can arise with the complexities of Medicaid managed care. Most can be handled by some phone calls and maybe some meetings with state officials to re-assure them. But this all works better if a relationship of mutual trust and understanding has been cultivated and nurtured over a period of time. Sanctions and fines may still occur (sometimes these are automatic by state contract or depending on the severity of the issue). I am not advocating a trustworthy relationship as a means to avoid penalties or achieve a get out of jail free card, but as a means to sustaining a long-term contractual partnership. There will be difficulties encountered and they come in surprising forms. For example, I know of at least two CEOs who consistently did the right thing, said the right things, took their lumps and bad days and found there was little upside (in their perspective) to this "relationship business." Their lament was the competing health plan that continuously failed to deliver, missed too many metrics, was difficult to deal with and yet remained contracted with the state and paid the same for their less-than-optimum performance. It can be disheartening and discouraging for those of us consistently going above and beyond. Life isn't fair and we have all witnessed the lazy or the incompetent get rewarded for failing to meet expectations. But we must do the right thing anyway; we must forge on and be the good partner to our states and manage operations appropriately. This is just one of those life lessons of acceptance and moving on.

Another difficulty is when there is a change in leadership, say at the governor level (which could impact who directs your Medicaid agency) or the Medicaid director themselves leaves for whatever reason and the new person has a disdain for you or your health plan or corporate organization (state agencies that are consistently hostile toward managed care plans are fortunately rare). Or perhaps there is a change in your own leadership and your boss/corporate office or even board of directors does not value relationships. Forge ahead and do it anyway. The benefits out-weigh the downside or risks.

In discussions with state Medicaid leaders, they have mentioned elements of what creates and sustains long-term relationships with contracted health plans, summarized in Table 5.1. The rest of this Chapter discusses how to accomplish this.

Table 5.1   What States Want from Health Plans

• Meet or exceed contractual requirements
• Keep them out of the newspapers; no negative headlines
• Advance their goals, as well as your own; it doesn't have to be either/or, it can be mutual and both sets of goals can be achieved
• Help them look good vis-a-vis other states
• Be good stewards of taxpayers' money
• No surprises

Read the Contract

So where does one start? Remember your overall goal is to be a trustworthy partner of your state's Medicaid agency and experience a mutually beneficial and long-lasting contractual relationship. So I always start with the contract itself (this assumes you already have a contract). The health plans I have worked with that achieved remarkable results all knew what was in their contract and had processes in place to ensure ongoing compliance. This was from the C-suite down to hourly employees, with appropriate governance by its board. Training on the contract requirements were generally tailored to the needs of the specific department, that is, Member Services knew the contractual requirements for member call center metrics (e.g., speed to answer), outreach, deadlines on identification card and benefit information mailings).

The takeaway is to read and understand your state contract and require the same from your direct reports. The most successful health plans provided training for their managers on the state contract. Follow this with the creation of structures (vis-a-vis Donabedian's approach) that provide the foundation to ensure the contract is followed and met. What does this look like? Here are some examples and suggestions.

Reporting

A good deal of your contractual requirements are regular reports that are due at specified times (e.g., monthly, quarterly). I've worked with health plans that didn't take this step too seriously and turned in incomplete and/or unreviewed reports, or turned them in later after asking (frequently) for due-date extensions. Of course state officials (senior leaders and directors of the affected functional areas, that is, finance, quality, compliance, member services) were irritated and quite often there were fines or other penalties exacted when there was failure to comply with turning reports in by a certain date. The remedy is deceptively simple. Turn them in on time. I say *deceptively* simple because you really need solid review processes and structural pieces in place to be successful. Here's what several health plans and organizations did to ensure ongoing compliance with reports submissions:

■ They set-up a spreadsheet schedule of reporting due dates, assigned staff ownership and responsibility for each report (e.g., employees/managers in quality, finance, medical).

- They built into the spreadsheet dates in advance to allow review of the report's data by senior leaders. This meant health plan management had appointments on their calendars for every month (or week) with the review times scheduled several days in advance of submission to the state.
- Any misses on expected outcomes revealed by the reports (e.g., length of stay, claims payment misses, misses on appeals turnaround times, call center metric misses) were identified and high-level action steps developed to address these deficiencies.
- The health plan then created a simple front sheet to accompany the state report that identified the health plan owner, report title, date, summary of findings and action plans initiated (if any; of course this is not necessary if the report metrics meet contractual requirements/expectations). This was successful in this state, so much so, the state requested other contracted health plans to do the same.
- Follow-through is necessary to ensure any actions taken make a difference in report outcomes, and the health plan made sure to keep the state informed of progress (or delays). Quite often this was simply done with the next report submission or next state meeting, as appropriate.

The process discussed signals to your state counterparts that you are actually reviewing the reports' findings (of whatever metric you are submitting), and understand them and are taking action to address any shortfalls. Did the state require this simple summary sheet? No, but they loved it and it was part of the many small steps this health plan took to restore trust.

This process meant a new commitment to health plan staff and leaders. It meant having reports ready at least a couple of days in advance and setting up meetings to review and develop action steps, if necessary. Were some reports reviewed and submitted just minutes before deadline? Yes. Things happen, but rather than the old method of forever submitting them late, incomplete or not even looked at, this became the exception and submitting complete, reviewed reports became the rule. Asking for extensions should be an exception as well. You are trying to build trust with your state and develop a partnership—submit on time, every time.

The other benefit to this health plan was the unexpected staff camaraderie that developed during these meeting times. Department leaders gathered to review reports for their respective areas in which good discussion ensued over misses or celebrations (yes, you need to celebrate), or over needed improvements. The process invoked teamwork and strengthened relationships within the health plan, boosting morale among these leaders.

Knowing your own health plan data and reporting results is as important as knowing your contract. I remember visiting another health plan in need of a turnaround—they were financially in trouble, had high employee turnover, high CEO turnover, and the state was ready to yank their multi-billion-dollar contract. My boss and I walked into the meeting room to gather with this health plan's CEO, COO, CMO, CFO, heads of medical services, compliance, etc. After greetings and pleasantries, we sat around the conference table and my boss asked one simple question: "how many heads in beds this morning (i.e., hospital census)?" The room became silent. The CMO and CEO looked at each other painfully and then around the room hoping someone on staff knew something. But no one knew anything. That short exchange told my boss and I everything we needed to know about where this health plan was at—they weren't even doing the most basic tasks of managed care daily discipline—knowing how many of your members were in the hospital. It was a major driver of their financial disarray. You can only know your data if you look at it and create the staff discipline to review and take action. This underscores the importance of an effective performance scorecard and monitoring processes.

Transparency and Disclosures

Earlier in Chapter 2, I talked about transparency as being a coveted characteristic of successful leaders. It means being easy to understand, open, not secretive and free from deceit. In your relationship with your state Medicaid agency, I extend this to disclosures, that is, the act of making something known or revealing something not previously known, such as informing your agency of missed contractual requirement(s). There are those who would be loathed to admit something was wrong, fearing sanctions or fines from their state. I say do the right thing and inform your state counterparts of any issues (e.g., loss of key provider contract, poorer results in a key metric than expected); give them a heads-up to avoid surprises. *Demonstrate to the state you are just as vested in protecting their reputation as your own.* If they are required to invoke a fine or sanction, accept it and move on. Better a fine and an intact relationship than a fine and a fractured relationship. Here is an example of what I mean.

I was in a meeting with a health plan's senior leaders and with a state's top Medicaid officials to review that health plan's steady improvement in key metrics, after years of poor results and an even poorer state relationship. We had successfully improved that relationship over a 12-month period by consistently demonstrating improvements in problematic areas (in this case, claims payments, appeals and turnaround times). The state officials sat there with beaming faces, pleased that our plan was on the right track with the recent performance reports. And then our CEO dropped a bombshell. On one of the reports that was of critical importance to the state, our CEO said he didn't believe the results. He thought there was something wrong with our IT systems, data was being miscounted and calculating a false positive result. The beaming faces disappeared. I cringed inwardly at the disclosure, unaware that our CEO had such suspicions. He quickly followed this revelation with his actions to address what he thought were inaccurate results (turns out he was right and the problem was eventually rectified). In place of the state official's beaming faces was first surprise, then relief and then a sense of deepening trust. The state staff appreciated the heads-up, the courage to admit something was wrong and the realization that a future report from us was going to show sub-par results. They had experienced years of receiving poor results from us with no fore-warning and they had long ago grown tired of being broadsided. Someone admitting in advance that something was wrong was new for them, and treasured. They encouraged us to disclose matters ahead of time, to lessen unpleasant surprises, though those are bound to occur over the length of a long-term contract.

Breadth and Depth of the Relationship

One turnaround adventure involved a struggling health plan that was approaching the renewal of its five-billion-dollar, five-year contract. The state Medicaid agency had been clear about its dissatisfaction with the performance of this health plan. In fact, the state's assistant directors and managers of different functional areas (such as quality, operations, medical services) did not hesitate to voice their utter frustration with this plan and their desire for it to be removed from the state. This group of mid-level state officials had no measure of trust with anyone at the health plan; there had been years of deteriorating performance by the plan leading to a broken relationship. Interestingly, the CEO of the health plan and the top state Medicaid official (the director, who reported to the governor) were close and enjoyed a somewhat friendly relationship, albeit stressed due to the plan's performance issues. Over time, it was becoming clear that these lingering performance issues were threatening the close relationship between these two. And consistently poor health plan performance was harming political relationships outside the state Medicaid agency (i.e., with legislators, the governor, provider organizations). It was also becoming clear, after spending time with the health plan mid-level managers, that no one else had a relationship with the state. It was all hinged on the two top people. And therein laid the larger problem. With the contract up for renewal via a competitive Request for Proposal process, guess who was going to read and score the RFP response and would be recommending to the Medicaid director which contractors should be awarded? Yes, the very mid-level managers at the state in which no one at the health plan had a relationship with. There were no regular meetings of mutual functional areas, or they were attended by lower level, inexperienced staff who didn't understand the state's continued distaste with the plan's performance. We were never going to re-procure that five-billion-dollar contract without repairing the relationship within the state Medicaid department and the only way to do that was to first improve our results and performance. Fortunately, this process was started a year in advance of their re-procurement. We set to work to address those deficiencies but the other step, in parallel, was to develop relationships with those state mid-level managers and demonstrate our actions and also to ask for help. Here, in more detail, are the steps we took:

- We asked each major health plan functional area to set-up regular meetings with their state counterpart (i.e., health plan quality staff with state quality staff, medical services, CMOs, CFOs, compliance), which could be weekly or monthly, depending on how much trouble those specific areas were in.
- They were to bring required reports and discuss with their state counterpart and encouraged to be open, ask questions and learn from the state. Most states, and I realize there are exceptions, were delighted to teach their contracted health plans what the state's expectations were and many willingly shared creative ideas on how to better meet contractual requirements.
- Health plan staff needed to bring back to health plan leaders feedback from the state, ideas for improvement, etc. This meant appropriate level health plan staff needed to be attending these meetings; they needed to have enough experience to recognize when the state was giving verbal and non-verbal messages of disapproval or impending sanctions or penalties.
- Health plan staff were required to follow-up on next steps—within the plan itself as well as with their state counterpart.

The breadth and depth of relationships extends and applies beyond just the Medicaid agency. It is imperative to establish relationships with your state's budget office, your governor's health policy advisor, legislators who participate on health policy committees, etc. These relationships can be owned by a board chair or other influential member or your CEO, CMO and/or a government relations person, depending on the size of your health plan.

This all contributes to my notion of the breadth and depth of the state Medicaid relationship. "Breadth" means across the multiple functional areas of the Medicaid agency, as in the director of quality, director of finance, director of compliance, etc. As well as "depth," meaning going down deep, vertically into the organization so that assistant directors, managers, assistant managers, supervisors and coordinators all know their health plan counterparts. It is important to know *what* you are working on to improve (relevant to their area of expertise); know *who* is accountable, and *how* to get hold of that person. Overall, it is important to cultivate relationships with top, middle and lower management at your state Medicaid department and other relevant state government offices.

Communications

One of the key improvements installed in several struggling health plans was a communication strategy with the main customer—the state Medicaid agency. Too often the state officials complained of unreturned phone calls or emails and lack of follow-up to either one.

I was inspired by a senior executive I had worked for years ago who had implemented the following strategies to help strengthen the relationship with a federal agency in which our company had a multi-billion-dollar contract. Here are some of those strategies, or relationship standards, tailored to and applied by Medicaid health plans for their states:

■ Acknowledging all calls and/or emails from the state within 24 (business) hours. If the answer to their inquiry was quickly at hand, we provided it. Quite often the state's call required some research on the health plan's part, so their communication was simply acknowledged and we provided some idea of when a full response would be given (if known at that time) or if the state set their own deadline, that of course would need to be met or negotiated.

■ We created a relationship grid to streamline and simplify (and in some cases clarify) who owned what relationship between the health plan and state Medicaid agency staff. This grid, an internal tool, matched up health plan functional area leaders with their state counterparts. For example, the CFO was responsible for owning the relationship with the state's finance director. This was mapped from the CEO (and board level, if applicable) down to compliance officers, quality directors, the CMO, all senior leader positions and most mid-level positions as well. Everyone embarked on establishing a relationship that entailed setting up regular meetings, sharing data, asking questions and striving to meet contractual requirements and expectations. The grid format also streamlined the number of touchpoints between the state and the health plan, clarified who was accountable for each functional area and how to contact them. Most states require that health plans provide contact information for key positions; creating for them an easy access spreadsheet for the state's internal use helps them know who notify for different functional areas. Health plan executives met regularly to review this relationship grid tool to assess its functionality and status of each relationship (i.e., going well, needs improvement). Furthermore, it helped control the communication tone and messages to the state, which lessened rumors, misinformation and confusion. Narrowing the number of people involved in interacting with your state officials helps to minimize chaotic communications and demonstrates to the state an increased ability to manage your own affairs.

■ The CEO was accessible to all, as needed. In addition, the CEO provided oversight of the overall relationship management program, regularly evaluating the activities sited and discussed previously. Some states asked for one contact person for the majority of inquiries and that generally fell to the compliance officer, who kept track of incoming requests from the state, the 24-hour acknowledgement, initial assignment of the accountable owner(s) of the request and the status (i.e., closed, pending). A simple spreadsheet captured this information and it was reviewed at weekly senior management meetings to ensure no issue fell through the cracks.

■ Some relationships are shared, for example, a government affairs staff person may also be meeting with the Medicaid director along with the health plan CEO as well as health care associations, legislators, governor's office and health policy advisor, state budget officer, etc. Keep in mind the breadth and depth of relationships mentioned earlier.

Written Communications

Formal, written communications to your state partner, whether electronic or hard copy, need to be treated as a relationship opportunity, just as much as everyday communications by phone or face-to-face. I recall a health plan, at risk of losing its contract due to chronic operational issues and misses, was responding via letter to the state's recent—and severe—sanction on the health plan. The initial letter drafted read as a stiff, cold, calculated legal briefing. The tone was adversarial without a hint of remorse and a weak attempt to avoid the charges and sanction (there was overwhelming evidence against the health plan). We had amassed an experienced team to turnaround this health plan and the senior leaders were ready, admittedly with some trepidation, to release this letter to the state, which I knew would only exacerbate an already tenuous situation. I intervened and was able to persuade the health plan leaders that this was a relationship opportunity and the road to improving the state's relationship with us—and preserving our chances of keeping a contract—could be furthered by responding with a different letter. The letter I recommended was one that communicated acknowledgement of the issue and our role in it, our commitment to the state and to Medicaid (this had come into question) and our desire to meet with the state to review our action plans, due dates and persons accountable to address the sanctioned issue. The overall tone of the letter was humble yet earnest and straightforward. And rather than having the health plan's lawyer signing the letter—which would have signaled to the state a potential legal battle and put both parties on the defensive—this version was signed by the CEO. The health plan was clearly in the wrong and trying to fight the state's action would only exacerbate a difficult relationship. Keep in mind the end goal—a long-term partnership built on trust and respect; and short-term, winning the upcoming RFP. Shifting this health plan's approach with the state was part of the beginning of the journey of improving communication, performance and the overall relationship—which blossomed in a positive way in a much shorter time than anyone had imagined.

Attitudinal and Non-Verbal Communications

I'm not sure why some health plans approach their state Medicaid agencies as adversaries, opposing nearly everything the state desires to achieve. It all goes much smoother and easier approaching them as partners (when your plan's performance warrants such a relationship), working together to improve the health and well-being of Medicaid beneficiaries. I'm not saying it's easy, or that there won't be times that opposing them is the thing to do. I'm applying a broad-brush stroke over the Medicaid relationship as one with respect and dignity for the person working at the state agency. I've heard derogatory comments about government workers from one of my own staff and cautioned him on this attitude and underlying hubris. My colleague's comment was tied to the time-worn, and inaccurate belief, that government workers are lazy and/or work shorter hours since they have fewer responsibilities. It's all not true and such conceit is easily conveyed to your state partners with less than desirable results. Treat them and your own employees with respect. You want to be able to meet regularly with your state partners and develop trust and mutual respect, which will only happen with frequent interactions, delivering on your commitments and keeping your promises.

There's also a trap to avoid in your relationship with your state partners, and that is the lure of offering states the "next big thing" in Medicaid. The newest, greatest solution to member non-compliance, or lowering no-show rates, or improving this or that. The trap is wanting to impress the state with your new ideas when your overall performance metrics fail to meet state standards. I've witnessed many executives attracted to the "shiny new thing" out there in Medicaid without first addressing the main issues the state wants resolved with your performance. Before you can have any credibility in bringing innovation and creativity to your state partner, you must first demonstrate you can deliver on the basics—pay the claims on time, meet turnaround times on appeals, meet call center standards for providers and members, etc. This also means consistently reviewing metrics and searching for OFIs (i.e., applying Kaizen principles), creating activities to address those opportunities, implementing them and evaluating their success. Demonstrating to your state the ability to do this effectively will quickly open the doors to more creative discussions.

Measuring Effectiveness

A relationship can be evaluated and measured just like any of your health plan's operational areas. From a simple "how are we doing?" at a joint face-to-face meeting or a more complex survey distributed to key leaders at your state's agency. I have seen great value in knowing how the state views you and feels about its relationship with you. Successful health plans regularly and objectively measure how they are performing from the state's perspective. Are you meeting state expectations? Have you asked them? Actually having this conversation can be very enlightening; some examples follow.

What to Measure

If you've been involved in Medicaid managed care for any length of time, you know that there are a lot of report submissions and a lot of data sharing. Most of it is useful to management of your operations and to state oversight, and admittedly, some of it is not and makes you wonder who looks at it and why do it. Rather than bemoan what doesn't make sense, work with your state to create reports that do work, for the benefit of all (i.e., your health plan, even your competitors, but mostly the state). This is in the spirit of creating a lasting relationship with your state and establishing a partnership role rather than an adversarial one. As mentioned previously, for those reports submitted to the state, ensure a thorough process of review and action needed to address any shortfalls. Establish regular meetings with your state to review key reports and verify you are on the same page (and avoid the contract loss and surprise exit of a large Midwest health plan mentioned below).

These contractually required metrics, however, tell only part of the story. They need to be balanced with other effectiveness measures of a health plan to determine its level of overall success, such as:

■ Employee satisfaction surveys
■ Member satisfaction surveys
■ Provider satisfaction surveys
■ Financial performance and the performance of any sub-contractors

An additional measure is surveying the state itself and asking them some simple questions—how satisfied are they with your health plan? Would they recommend you to another state? Many CEOs are terrified to ask their state these kind of questions, afraid of the answer and the work involved in addressing less than a positive response. It is helpful, though, not only for garnering feedback that could make a big difference in your overall state relationship, but it is frequently a RFP question. Many managed care states that procure Medicaid contracts through a competitive bid process ask for references from other states (applicable if you are a multi-state Medicaid organization). Quite often, states will ask for a list of all contracts and contact people and they will choose who to reach out to for feedback—wouldn't you want to know what each state would say and have the opportunity to address any less-than-stellar answers in your RFP response? That is, to be able to describe in the RFP response what may have gone wrong in another state and what was (or is) being done about it. The intent here is to stay ahead of potentially harmful feedback and a negative impact on your RFP results. You may not always be able to get quantitative survey results from your state(s), but establish with your state regular contract reviews, performance evaluations, identification of OFIs, and implementation plans to address shortfalls, etc. and begin the process of openly discussing your performance as a health plan.

I know of a Medicaid managed care organization that took steps in measuring effectiveness and obtaining state feedback. The organization set to work in developing a robust survey instrument that would measure states' satisfaction across several functional areas, such as claims, quality, provider and member services, reports, etc. The survey results were reviewed by senior health plan executives and OFIs were identified and addressed. The survey included the simple question—How likely are you to refer them to another state? Responses ranged on a scale from "not satisfied" to "very satisfied," or "not likely" to "very likely."

This organization was contracted with over 20 states and collecting this data provided invaluable information to help improve their operational performance but also to strengthen their state relationships. The "how likely" question is similar to the Net Promoter Score popularized by Richard Owen and Dr. Laura Brooks' book *Answering the Ultimate Question* in which they advocate a similar question (and others) to act on customer feedback in order to optimize your company's results (see *netpromoter.com*). The results this organization collected were for the most part expected—the result of a great effort to establish good relationships with all of their state Medicaid agencies and continuously improve their performance. But there were surprises which immediately provided some eye-opening state discussions. For example, there was a state that the company met with extensively and was confident of a solid relationship and yet, the state scored the company much lower on the "how likely" question than expected. Within the year, the multi-billion-dollar contract was going to bid; this was not the time to score low on this question. Since a relationship between the state and the plan already existed, it allowed the plan to meet with the state and probe with additional questions, specifically, what led the state to score them so low? The state's response was illuminating and set the health plan into motion to address remaining issues, which had the effect of improving future satisfaction scores, the health plan's overall performance and also solidified an already good relationship into a great one.

Two anecdotes stand out in my mind about the importance of measuring your effectiveness, consistently identifying OFIs and addressing them and nurturing a sustainable state relationship.

A medium-sized Midwestern health plan, part of a national Medicaid company, had just completed its RFP response for a re-procurement of their state contract. Everyone, including me and my colleagues at corporate head-quarters, had been assured of success with the RFP response. "The state loves us …" enthused its CEO, "I have a great relationship with them." The RFP team was pleased with their product and all was well until we learned we had lost the entire state. We were stunned. Fast forward to corpo-rate executives parachuting in for meetings with state Medicaid officials to find out what happened. "We can't stand you guys, in particular the CEO" remarked one of the key state leaders. In fact, there was no "great relation-ship"; the CEO had isolated himself and his staff when things had started to go bad. He had solely owned the state relationship responsibility (i.e., no breadth or depth) and had bungled it badly. Corporate equally had misfired in applying appropriate oversight of this plan. There were also some RFP scoring issues, which turned out to be our saving grace as it allowed us to remain in the state while the RFP was re-issued and we had time to initiate turnaround efforts (which were eventually successful). The stress involved in this process, though, could have been avoided with having first established the breadth and depth of a state relationship and measuring its effectiveness.

Another Midwest health plan, larger in membership than the previous example, had also just submitted its RFP response for contract re-procure-ment. They were equally positive of their great RFP submission and chances of award. In their response, they had touted and sang their own praises over the improvements they had made in operational areas the state had been penalizing them for missing. The health plan listed their metrics in the RFP response, demonstrating vast improvement. Unfortunately, their data didn't match what the state had. In the state's eyes, the health plan was still miss-ing performance standards and this contributed to losing the RFP re-pro-curement and their contract. To their chagrin, the health plan did not have a relationship with the state Medicaid agency. Such a relationship would have included mutually reviewing performance metrics and agreeing with what was measured, how often and a thorough evaluation and agreement on the results. Any discrepancies uncovered during this process could have been rectified prior to the RFP being issued. These kind of meetings would have avoided what ended up to be a great embarrassment to the health plan in addition to the elimination of jobs and financial losses.

Repairing Broken State Relationships

The whole idea of this book was borne out of my experience in turning around health plans whose state relationships and performance were so bad that any chance of survival seemed hopeless. As mentioned previously, these health plans all shared similar attributes:

- Poor performance on a variety of metrics: Claims payment, appeals turnaround times, member services, provider services, quality management, finance, etc. or in severe cases, all of the above.
- Member complaints (either revealed in satisfaction surveys or calls to the state agency).
- Frequent provider complaints (many going directly to the state Medicaid director or even the governor because of lack of response from the health plan).
- Persistent dissatisfaction from the state with chronic complaints and threats of contract cancellation.
- Repeated sanctions and penalties.
- Habitual employee dissatisfaction and high employee turnover rate.
- Poor financial performance.
- Infrequent or ineffective meetings with state Medicaid officials.
- Relationship, if one exists, is only held by one-person, frequently the CEO with the state Medicaid director; little to no relationship deep into either organization (no breadth or depth).
- Arrogance and hubris from health plan leadership (and sometimes other staff); an attitude that they could do no wrong or were smarter than the state. This behavior was often a harbinger of a failing state relationship even before performance metrics reflected shortfalls.
- They also shared one other important attribute (after interventions): *They all turned around and survived.*

The tasks ahead, to repair not only the health plans' functioning but the state relationship and to reduce the risk of losing these contracts seemed impossible. It prompted one talented executive brought in for a turnaround to remark in despair "I just want to flee." Each health plan, however, did turnaround, restored operational effectiveness and financial integrity, retained their contracts and most importantly re-established trustworthy and mutually satisfactory relationships with their state Medicaid agencies. In each case, I awaited what was for me the hallmark of a successful turnaround (even if we weren't quite done yet)—it was hearing the words from state officials "you are on the right track now ... we don't need to meet with you so often anymore." Another one was the state reaching out to the health plan for help on another matter. It meant they looked to us as helpful, having expertise, that we were knowledgeable and trustful partners. This signaled to me and my colleagues that we had turned the corner and were on our way and had successfully achieved our goals.

It did require diligence, commitment and tireless effort to deliver on promises. And everyone involved in these massive turnaround efforts sure wished these big messes had never been created in the first place. Steps taken involved:

- Reaching out to state officials and asking for meetings to openly discuss performance miscues.
- Demonstrating humility, transparency and consistency on the health plan's part, even if not reciprocated by the state. Always conduct yourself with dignity, trustworthiness and humility and treat your state counterparts the same way. Don't be afraid to ask for help. Most state Medicaid staff are delighted to help their health plans be successful. Remember, it serves no one well to have a health plan fail.
- Ensuring depth and breadth of the state relationships (as described earlier in this chapter).
- Meeting regularly with state officials to review data reports and outcomes in detail and *mutually* agree on improvements and/or areas still in need of improvement.

It can also be helpful to revisit your mission, vision and values statements, to make sure what you are doing is in alignment with those and with the state's. This is why I emphasized this in Chapter 1. It can be a great way to hit re-start with you, your staff and your state and recommit yourself to why you are in this business.

One health plan set-up biweekly meetings with their state and developed detailed reports with the raw data summarized into charts and figures that visually showed the impact of improvements. The state was impressed, not only with the health plan's attention to issues but the reports themselves that were eventually adopted by the state and used for all their contracted health plans.

Digging out of deep trouble with your state is not the ideal situation. It's time consuming, resource intensive, stressful and risky. There's no guarantee that all the improvements and restoration of relationships will result in becoming a reference account or in retaining a contract. Even if you leave a state—for whatever reason—restoring or retaining a state relationship can be part of future successes in other states or upon returning to the state you left.

Summary of Key Points

- Develop a systematic approach to lasting relationships; create a plan, work and measure it and evaluate its effectiveness.
- Treat and work with your state as a partner and seek to delight your state partner.
- Read and understand your contractual requirements.
- Create culture and internal structures to consistently deliver on promises and meet or exceed state requirements.
- Establish relationships across the breadth and depth of your health plan (including board members, C-level staff, etc.) and state Medicaid agency; meet regularly.
- Model humility, trustworthiness, integrity.
- Disclose to state any potential misses (remember, no surprises and protect their reputation as well as your own) and be good stewards of the state's (and taxpayers') money.
- Advance your state partner's mission and goals along with your own.
- Measure, monitor, evaluate and address shortfalls.
- Establish trust first before embarking on the "next big thing."

Chapter 6

Sustaining Success

Successful organizations are able to sustain their success not because they are able to avoid operational or financial mishaps or external challenges, but because they are able to respond to those challenges and emerge as a stronger, more effective entity. Medicaid managed care health plans are no different. There will be plenty of operational or financial hiccups in any Medicaid health plan's life-cycle.

In a recent interview with Berkshire Hathaway's Warren Buffett, Mr. Buffett describes his philosophy on investing in companies that experience scandals or operational/financial mishaps. He doesn't abandon companies when problems occur, but he does expect that those problems are handled responsibly. He invested in these companies "because we thought they had very, very strong hands" (Frankel 2017). In other words, there was a level of trust and a strong enough relationship that gave Mr. Buffett confidence those investments would someday pay off, despite some hurdles. The process of developing that trust indicated that the leadership and governance of the company was solid and strong and the organization was committed to its purpose. This is the level of leadership and governance, and commitment to one's mission, vision and values, covered in Chapters 1 and 2 that you want to achieve with your own health plan. A similar level of trust and relationship can be created with your state Medicaid agency. They are investing in you and expect any problems to be dealt with responsibly. You don't want them divesting in you, which in this scenario could mean not re-contracting with your health plan or imposing sanctions or fines.

Changes in leadership will also occur: at the corporate level, which may impact your health plan; at the government level, which may impact your relationship with the affected state agency; or changes to your own leader-ship team, which means hiring new leaders or promoting from within. How you respond to these changes and challenges determines a lot about your longevity in sustaining success. And a good dose of passion for the work you do in Medicaid managed care. It's this passion and sense of purpose, along with a systematic approach to leading the health plan, that creates sustainable success. Continue to ask yourself how you can delight your state Medicaid agency partners. It's done by meeting contractual requirements, creating a systematic approach to nurturing relationships with key stakeholders (i.e., community organizations, legislators, in addition to state Medicaid personnel) and limiting surprises with appropriate transparency and disclosures.

An unappreciated element in all of this is the application of creativity and innovation, in problem-solving to address challenges, as well as in develop-ing brand new ideas. There has been a larger emphasis around new models of care and intervention. "States are looking for managed care companies to examine new possibilities for engagement, use of social determinants as an aid in health care management and new tools (e.g., digital interventions)" explained Rick Jelinek, Executive Vice President at Aetna Inc (January 2017, personal communication, with permission). Developing and sharing with your state officials these new health care innovations can be thrilling and professionally rewarding. Discussions with your state partner can revolve around new innovations and best practices that are being tested or imple-mented in other markets. Getting to the table to have these discussions means a level of trust and a meaningful relationship already exists.

Earlier I mentioned one of the hallmarks of knowing when you were succeeding in turning around your health plan: when your state was ready to say to you "you're on the right track" or "we don't need to meet as often anymore"—a sign of deepening trust. Another hallmark is when your state reaches out to you for help. They seek you out as thought leader(s) on tough health care concerns (e.g., addressing infant mortality in your state) or leg-islative issues (e.g., the state Medicaid budget). The state approaching you for help or promoting the notion of partnership to solve a common health challenge in your state is one of the highest compliments paid and is a sign of trust and true partnership. Your underlying goal has been to be a trusted partner that is willing and able to advance your state's mission and vision, as well as your own, for the betterment of society's most vulnerable people and for the common good of Medicaid beneficiaries.

Trust and relationships has been stressed so much in this book because of its foundational importance in sustaining success in leading your Medicaid health plan. Developing trust with your state Medicaid officials takes time and relentless dedication. And you also have to be simultaneously building trust with other stakeholders—providers, community organizations, your employees, etc. Trust comes with risks and those risks must also be managed by you as described in Chapter 4. For example, your state Medicaid agency is trusting you to fulfill your contractual obligations and they managed that risk in part by imposing sanctions or fines when requirements are not met consistently. Likewise, your sub-contractors, who you trust to perform health plan activities to your contractual specifications, should be held accountable to meet those requirements, or experience penalties for failure to do so. Managing your risks, within the context of retaining trust, becomes an important component of sustaining success.

The crux of the previous five chapters was largely based on building a strong foundation (vis-a-vis Donabedian's model) and infrastructure of mission/vision/values; a sense of purpose that provides a true north and guiding principles for your health plan. It is also recognizing the symmetry of health plan mission/vision/value statements with those of the state Medicaid agency and aligning those visions into a partnership that seeks to meet mutual goals.

This foundation or structure extends to governance and health plan leadership, choosing leaders who are diverse and representative of the people served by your health plan. And health plan executives who are humble rather than dazzling, and able to create a culture of focused discipline around relationship building and meeting contractual requirements.

It's the ability to lead the organization through effective strategic planning steps that strive to meet/exceed contractual requirements while advancing the goals of the state, as well as those of your own organization. And meeting with the state to ensure intents are understood and health plan performance meets the state's expectations.

All this structure and foundational work must be implemented via processes that integrate provider, member, community and employee relationships and work products. That is, none of these areas should work in a vacuum.

Finally, this culminates in Chapter 5 with the state relationship itself, in which relationship development and cultivation can and should be strategized, planned, documented, evaluated and adjusted as needed. It means regularly meeting with your state Medicaid agency leaders, governor's office, budget office, legislative health care committee members, influential community leaders, organizations and advocates and others and continuously asking: "how are we doing?" "What can we do better?" "Are we meeting your needs?" "What can we do—together—to better improve the health of our state's most vulnerable individuals and keep costs manageable?" It means knowing and understanding your state Medicaid contract(s) and having a relentless focus on measuring results and adjusting processes as needed. It means not surprising or embarrassing your partners at the state, with whom you have worked hard to earn their trust. This means respecting them and acknowledging—however you or your colleagues may resist—that they are the ones paying you and entrusting you to operate ethically, lawfully and to the best of your ability. Honor this dynamic, as it may be tenuous at times, but in the long run, respect and preserving the dignity of your state partners will enhance your ability to sustain success.

At the beginning I said this is all hard work, but it is also worthwhile and rewarding. When you see the fruits of your efforts in good performance results, (e.g., trustworthy relationship with your state agency, improved member outreach statistics, lower hospital re-admission rates, high provider satisfaction scores), or a state leader comes to you to ask for your help because they see you and your organization as thought leaders, then you know you are on the right track. Staying on the right track takes determination, focus and a bit of good luck. But most importantly, it means cultivating and sustaining a mutually respectful relationship with your state partners.

Summary of Key Points

- Developing trustful relationships takes time and effort and meeting contract requirements is the first step.
- Manage risks and deal with operational difficulties responsibly to retain that level of trust.
- Continue to bring best practices and innovation to your state, while pursuing a common purpose.
- Integrate the elements of trustful relationships and shared missions with meeting contractual requirements for long-lasting and sustained success.

References

Abrahams, J. (1999). *The Mission Statement Book*. Berkeley, CA: Ten Speed Press.

Centers for Medicare and Medicaid Services. Center for Strategic Planning. (2012). "Financial Performance of Health Plans in Medicaid Managed Care," by Mike McCue. *Medicare and Medicaid Research Review 2012,* Volume 2, Number 2. Washington, DC.

Collins, J. (2001). *Good to Great*. New York: HarperCollins.

Donabedian, A. (1980). *The Definition of Quality and Approaches to Its Assessment*. Ann Arbor, MI: Health Administration Press.

Egan, T. (2017, April 8). The soul of a corporation. *New York Times*, p. A25.

Frankel, M. (2017, May 8). Five key takeaways from Berkshire Hathaway chat. *Arizona Republic*, p. 4B.

Goleman, D. (2000). *Working with Emotional Intelligence*. New York: Bantam.

Green, C. (2012, April 3). Why trust is the new core of leadership. *Forbes*, p. 1.

Jelinek, R. (2017, January 3). Personal communication.

Henry J. Kaiser Family Foundation. (2015, July). *State Health Facts.* Available at: http://www.kff.org/interactive/medicaid-state-fact-sheets/

Larson, J. (2015). *Oversight & Wisdom*. W. P. Carey School of Business Magazine, pp. 18–19. Tempe, AZ: Arizona State University.

Medicaid Health Plans of America. (2016, July). *Our Mission*. Available at: http://www.medicaidplans.org/about-mhpa/our-mission.

Paradise, J., Lyons, B. and Rowland, D. (2015, May). *Medicaid at 50*. Kaiser Commission on Medicaid and the Uninsured. Available at: www.kff.org.

Senn, L. and Hart, J. (2010). *Winning Teams, Winning Cultures*. Second Edition. Long Beach, CA: Senn Delaney.

Wertheimer, M. (2013). *The Board Chair Handbook*. Third Edition. Washington, DC: BoardSource.

Resources

Here is a list of helpful organizations and readings. I recommend being familiar with the ones dedicated to Medicaid and/or vulnerable populations. They contain a wealth of information every Medicaid executive should be acquainted with.

BoardSource: Inspires and supports excellence in non-profit governance and board and staff leadership. www.boardsource.org

Center for Health Care Strategies: Advancing innovations in health care delivery for low-income Americans. www.chcs.org

Improving Corporate Governance with the Balanced Scorecard: Harvard Business School, Robert S. Kaplan and Michael E. Nagel, www.hbs.edu.

Kaiser Family Foundation: A leader in health policy analysis and health journalism dedicated to trusted information on health issues. www.kff.org

Kaizen Institute: Continuous improvement as an important pillar of an organization's long-term competitive strategy. www.kaizen.com

Kongstvedt, P. (2012). *Essentials of Managed Health Care*. Burlington, MA: Jones and Bartlett Learning.

Medicaid Health Plans of America: The leading trade association solely focused on representing Medicaid health plans. www.medicaidplans.org

National Association of Corporate Directors: Recognized authority on leading boardroom practices. www.nacdonline.org

National Association of Medicaid Directors: Independent, bipartisan association of those who oversee Medicaid in all 50 states, District of Columbia and US territories. www.medicaiddirectors.org

National Association of State Budget Officers: Advancing state budget practices through research, policy analysis, education and knowledge. www.nasbo.org

Net Promoter Network: www.netpromoter.com

The CommonWealth Fund: Promotes high-performing health care system focused on society's most vulnerable. www.commonwealthfund.org

Index